The Great CYCLE

Predicting and Profiting from Crowd Behavior, the Kondratieff Wave, and Long-Term Cycles

REVISED EDITION

Dick Stoken

PROBUS PUBLISHING COMPANY
Chicago, Illinois
Cambridge, England

ISBN 1-55738-487-8

Printed in the United States of America

BB

2 3 4 5 6 7 8 9 0

TAQ/BJS

To:

Sandra Loebe, Antigone, Kingsley,

Andre & Deidre

with Love

TABLE OF CONTENTS

● ● ● ● ● ●

Table of Contents

Acknowledgments
• • • • • •

My special gratitude to:

Gary Crossland for many valuable contributions which included preparing the charts, reading parts of the manuscript and numerous helpful suggestions.

Haskel Benishay for his advice in the first edition of this book.

Antigone Stoken for a superb job of editing and many helpful suggestions to enrich the content of this book.

Kingsley Stoken for the painstaking task of typing portions of this book.

Sandra Loebe for her many suggestions and inspiration.

Thanks for helping make this book what it is.
I could not have traveled the distance without you.

"A prophet is one who, when everyone else despairs, hopes. And when everyone else hopes, he despairs. You'll ask why. It's because he has mastered the great secret: **The Wheel Turns.**"

Sly Thomas in Nikos Kazantzakis'
The Last Temptation of Christ
(Simon & Schuster, New York, 1960.)

THE WHEEL TURNS: AN INTRODUCTION TO THE LONG CYCLE

• • • • • •

In 1990 a recession struck—a fairly mild contraction according to statistical measures. However, unlike in the eight other post World War II recoveries the economy has not gotten back on a fast growth track. In fact it took an interminably long time to even regain its footing. The Fed did its bit and pushed short term interest rates down from 7½ percent to 5 percent to 4 percent and finally to under 3 3 percent. Still, . . . the economy appears stuck in the mud.

1

Chapter One

Middle class incomes are falling, living standards are threatened, and a pervasive feeling of anxiety has spread across the land.

This situation sounds eerily familiar to the economists and Wall Streeters who follow in the footsteps of Nikolai Kondratieff, a Russian economist. Back in the 1920s, Kondratieff noticed that since the start of the industrial revolution capitalist economies have experienced long waves of growth and contraction. According to Kondratieff, 25- to 35-year waves of increasing prosperity and living standards are followed by a decade or more of depression, during which factories lay idle, crops go unharvested and legions of the working class lose their jobs and become demoralized. These severe economic upheavals come at fairly regular 45- to 60-year intervals. As Kondratieff explained it, these great tides in economic affairs—so-called secular trends—will, of course, have temporary setbacks, known as recessions. However these setbacks are generally mild and are soon followed by another surge of business activity, resulting in a new peak in economic output.

Kondratieff's theory suggests that depressions will rid a capitalist economy of its excesses so that it can rise again from the ashes like a Phoenix and begin a new burst of industrial growth. His Soviet superiors did not appreciate the consequences of this theory, but Kondratieff did not back down. Shortly thereafter he was packed off to Siberia, never to be heard from again. Nevertheless, his ideas crossed the Atlantic Ocean and were embraced by a small but respectable fringe group of economists, most notably Schumpeter, Forrester, and Rostow.

Most economists are skeptical of Kondratieff's theory. They do not believe economic activity occurs in cycles. They question why economic growth should be discontinuous. They do not understand that cycles in economic activity are rooted in the way people relate to their world. Just as a powerful gravitational pull between the heavenly bodies holds our solar system in place, a powerful sociobiological pull keeps economic trends on course. Let me clarify.

Imagine a group of animals which feeds on one type of insect. As long as the insects are plentiful, the animals have plenty of food and they multiply. However, as their population grows the insects become pretty well eaten up, depleting the animals' source of food. Naturally, the animals begin dying off, enabling the insect population to grow. Just when the animals face extinction, an increasing supply of insects provides a source of food so that the animals can multiply once again. Over periods of time, the animal population fluctuates from large to small to large. Just as the animal population affects and is affected by the population of the insects it feeds upon, the desire to be a risk taker, both affects and is affected by the alternating states of prosperity and depression in the economy.

Risk Takers and Risk Averters

Risk takers are those who attempt to feed off or benefit from a growing economy. Though generally thought of as profit seekers, such as entrepreneurs and speculators, they might also include those who borrow in order to improve their standard of living. Risk averters, on the other hand, are not willing to depend upon an expanding economy for their well-being. They are usually people who prefer the security of a steady paycheck, such as salaried employees, but may also include those who delay consumption so as to build up their savings. These two categories describe a general tendency to either extend or not extend one's economic commitments.

These behavioral tendencies create cycles of economic activity. What happens is that during prosperity people come to believe their economic prospects will continue to improve, increasing their desire to become risk takers. Entrepreneurs expand their economic commitments and consumers are not afraid to take on debt in order to increase their standard of living. This behavior in turn fuels the economic expansion. However, as this economic trend continues on an upward slope, risk takers become more numerous. When too many participants in the economy become risk takers, the supply of economic goods expands and reaches levels that outstrip demand. It is necessary to alter behavior so that some people become risk averters; that is, they stop borrowing money, stop building economic commitments, and increase their work effort. In order for this to happen, people must experience some economic pain, such as a recession. Thus, just as night follows day, expansions are followed by contractions which in turn are followed by renewed expansion.

The relationship between the desire to be a risk taker and the state of the economy produces a long economic cycle of expansion and retrenchment. An extended period of prosperity increases the value of assets and the standard of living well beyond what most people expect. They have experienced a lesson of pleasure. The experience of economic pleasure produces a definite psychological change in most people. Over 200 years ago, the British philosopher, Jeremy Bentham said, "Nature has placed man under the governance of two sovereign masters, pain and pleasure. It is for them alone to point out what we shall do."

After experiencing economic prosperity, people see the world as less risky and this induces a fundamental change in their behavior. The pleasure principle takes over. People attain a healthy optimism and are more willing to strike out in new directions and take on new ventures. That is, people are more willing to start new business firms, make new investments, take on debt, or increase consumption. This behavior provides a tremendous lift to the economy.

The prevailing state of mind also provides an underlying source of support to the economy so that a business slump does not feed upon itself, and become a depression. There is an ample number of risk takers waiting in the wings to take advantage of the falloffs in the cost of capital and labor that typically occur during a business slump, and increase their investments. Also, consumers will not cut expenditures materially because their long-term outlooks are favorable. Instead, they dip into savings or take on debt in order to maintain their standard of living. The result is a long period of expansion. During this expansionary phase of the cycle, business contractions will be brief and mild, and each expansion in business activity easily surpasses the level achieved at the peak of the preceding expansion. Furthermore, during this time the growing demand for goods and credit leads to rising wholesale prices and interest rates.

Chapter One

An Error of Optimism

However, after about a generation of extraordinary increases in living standards and profits, people lose touch with reality. Large numbers of people think what happened in the past will continue indefinitely, and become risk takers. An influx of new entrepreneurs attempting to exploit the promising investment opportunities, combined with an enormous increase in expenditures by consumers, produces a hefty increase in the demand for credit. Long-term interest rates (the cost of capital) rise above the natural rate of interest. [The natural rate of interest is the theoretical rate of return on capital after adding in an allowance for inflation. Although economists have not been able to quantify the natural rate, if we average long-term interest rates over the last 150 years we get about a 3½ percent rate. Add to that an allowance for inflation, which in the decade preceding 1967 was about 2 percent and we could peg the natural rate in 1967 at approximately 5½ percent.] When risk takers pay more for money than the natural rate of interest, they commit an error of optimism. The reason: this army of new risk takers, produces an explosion in the demand for raw materials, agricultural products, fuel, and labor, which far outstrips supply. As business people furiously try to expand their productive capacity, prices for those goods are bid up, and the economy experiences raging inflation. The cost of doing business mounts at the very time that the soaring prices of food and energy are taking a bigger portion out of consumers' budgets. This leaves less money available to purchase industrial goods and all of the sudden the demand evaporates. A steep contraction is sure to follow.

However, this is not the end of the expansionary phase. The supply of goods is not permanently out of line with the demand, nor have the profitable investment opportunities been exhausted. Following a modest fall in the cost of doing business, another batch of risk takers arrives on the scene to build economic commitments. Business activity rebounds. Consumer demand perks up and this allows business people to raise prices, which will partially offset their high production costs, at least for a while. Yet, long-term interest rates remain stubbornly above the natural rate.

Uneven Growth During "Plateau Period"

This business rebound does not produce the widespread prosperity seen in the earlier years of the expansionary phase. There is about a decade of uneven growth that the Kondratieff groupies call the "plateau period." This is a transition period marked by mounting evidence of deep-seated difficulties such as increasing foreign and domestic competition, sagging productivity, declining profitably in older industries and, most important of all, an immense build-up of debt.

During this period, the profitable investment opportunities become exhausted, but the risk takers pay no heed. They are still optimistic and continue to take on new investment believing that consumers will put on their spending clothes. The result is a great deal of excess capacity along with a mountain of debt. New investment, undertaken at this time when business costs are high, unlike that initiated at the beginning of the expansionary

Chapter One

phase, puts corporate profitability in jeopardy. Competition intensifies. Many markets become saturated and business people find they can no longer raise prices to offset their increased costs. Profits begin to erode and the excess capacity and excessive debt can no longer be supported. They must be liquidated (see Figure 1–1).

The resulting contraction frightens a goodly number of the overextended risk takers. They begin liquidating debt, which triggers a domino-like pattern of bankruptcies and unemployment. The unexpected falloff in the value of people's assets, job security, and standard of living serves as a lesson of pain. People who have seen friends and relatives dragged down to hunger and want, now view the world as a pretty risky place. They become pessimistic about their economic future, creating a fundamental change in the way they act. Their focus shifts to avoiding pain and protecting themselves. Business executives terminate their operations, reduce debt, fire workers, and discontinue unprofitable ventures. At the same time, consumers postpone their purchases. The fact that huge numbers of people are lining up to shed their economic commitments acts as a weight on the economy.

Contractions can now feed upon themselves. They will no longer be mere pauses in a major expansion. Instead they are part of a major business retrenchment which is the depressionary or stagnant phase of this long cycle. This is a painful time of gut-wrenching structural change and great discontent. The wheel of fortune turns, and hundreds of thousands of people who had climbed their way onto lofty economic perches fall and hit the ground with a thud. They wake up to discover they had hitched their

Figure 1-1 Ideal Wave

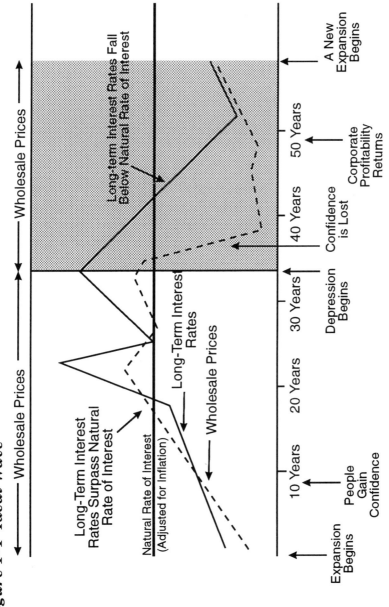

careers and savings to jobs and industries that had out-
lived their usefulness. There are, of course, periods of
cyclical expansion during the downward phase of the cycle, but they are apt to be sluggish and they will do little
to achieve the widespread prosperity necessary to alter
the controlling pessimism.

An Error of Pessimism

At this point, because people have become overly cautious,
savings increase and the demand for money lessens. Consequently, long-term interest rates slip back below the
natural rate of interest. People are now committing an
error of pessimism. The reason: the lack of risk takers also
produces a reduction in the demand for raw materials,
agricultural products, and labor which cheapens their
price, dramatically lowering business costs. Also, competition has been reduced, as excess capacity was weeded
out, and a backlog of unsatisfied consumer demand will
have developed. As a result, new business ventures will
soon be able to produce a favorable investment return.
When business activity does pick up there will be a sharp
rise in profits and the forces of expansion will be set in
motion once again. And so the cycle goes. We cannot
prevent this process from occurring because in capitalist
economies as in nature, there is an immutable law of
growth and decay operating.

Currently, it appears that the wheel of fortune has turned
down and two generations of Americans have no idea of
what living on the downslope of the Kondratieff cycle is
like. This book will show you what a downswing is like and
tell you how to cope with this new environment. Investors

without knowledge of this long cycle have difficulty putting events in historical perspective. They are like soldiers on one field of battle who, upon seeing the enemy retreat, think the war is being won, while in truth the decisive battle is being fought somewhere else and their opponents are winning it. On the other hand, investors who understand this long cycle, become like the generals on the hill, observing all the battles, hence more likely to accurately predict the outcome of the war. As Adam Smith said in *The Money Game,* "You do have to know what time of market it is. Markets go in cycles like all the other rhythms of life."

As is explained in greater detail in Chapter Thirteen, there are typically five long bull markets during each cycle, wherein the value of stocks and other assets show dramatic increases. There have been eight such bull markets since 1896. This book will teach you how to spot these bull markets, as did its first edition. In the first edition, which was completed in 1978, I concluded that we were about to see "a return of political stability with a fiscal and social conservatism . . . (along with) a time of non inflationary economic growth. . . accompanied by a broad bull market in stocks." Further I stated that, "The Dow Jones Industrial Average, if it is to equal the rise . . . which occurred during the last expansionary period, . . . should sell at 2700." In 1987 the Dow achieved that level and has since risen well beyond it. Also, I will demonstrate that this long cycle is not quite the same as Kondratieff followers describe. Like most things, its nature keeps changing and Chapters Five and Fourteen will show how to spot these changes. Finally, in the course of this book we shall also see that this long cycle has a very important effect on all of us. This is because these long periods of prosperity and stagnation serve as lessons of pain or pleasure, which unleash

Chapter One

important but unseen psychological forces that influence the way we think and act in our social and political as well as our economic life.

Let us now study the anatomy of a Kondratieff cycle.

AN ANATOMY OF A CYCLE
● ● ● ● ● ●

In 1897, the United States economy emerged from a 24-year period of recurring depression, and began a long period of prosperity. New gold discoveries in South Africa, along with the Spanish-American War, touched off an inflation, which stimulated business activity and lifted the economy out of the mire of depression. The introduction and exploitation of cheap electric power helped generate a new phase of industrialization. Oil, which was plentiful and cheap, replaced coal as the chief fuel in this new energy system. Electric power reduced the costs of industries that used machinery; it precipitated a massive transformation of industrial plant; and generated a flood of durable consumer goods such as refrigerators, washing machines, and radios. The railroad industry, which had been the dominant industry during the preceding 40 years, was revived. The stock market began a long rise which would increase the Dow Jones Industrial Average by more than 1,800 percent over the next 33 years. Moreover, long-term interest rates and wholesale prices began a long uphill march, which, with brief interruptions, would last 21 years (see Figure 2–1).

The first decade of this expansion was a period of conformity accompanied by social tranquillity. Tranquillity typically occurs during this period of the cycle because people are not expecting as much and therefore are more easily satisfied. Consequently, when the economy improves, people don't want to rock the boat, so a great deal of social stability develops. Business profits were fairly easy to come by because the earlier depression had left a legacy of cheap capital and labor, as well as reduced competition. The inflation at the beginning of the cycle was easily cooled and the economy continued to expand. There were, of course, two recessions. Both, however, were mild, and confidence in the future of the economy soon returned. In general, people were pleased with the way things were going and did not want to rock the boat.

By 1906, evidence of the growing prosperity had shown up almost everywhere and people began to lose the caution bred by the depression. The stock exchanges were hit with a wave of speculation. Businesses increased the size of inventories and stepped up spending on capital items, which increased the need for labor and raw materials, putting upward pressure on the cost of labor and materials. A wave of borrowing put a strain on the banking system, which sent interest rates soaring. At the same

14

Figure 2-1 Interest Rates and Wholesale Prices (United States 1896–1992)

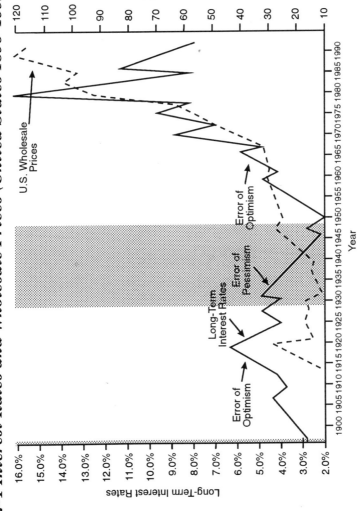

Source: *A History of Interest Rates*, Second Edition, by Sidney Homer, 1963, 1977 by Rutgers The State University of NJ. Reprinted by permission of Rutgers University Press.

time, competition increased so that it became difficult to raise prices and the economy became temporarily overextended.

The result was a serious recession in 1907, accompanied by the worst stock market break since the last depression, shaking the emerging confidence. Although this contraction was more serious than the previous two, it did not snowball into a depression as had happened in the early 1890s. The underlying business fundamentals were sound. The market for goods was not saturated. The overall level of debt was still moderate. Once people got the message that the economy was not as rosy as they had thought, they became more cautious, labor productivity rose, and capital became cheaper and more abundant. The upward march in long-term interest rates had been interrupted and the expansion resumed.

Age of the Automobile Arrives

As we recovered from this serious recession a new industry—automobile manufacturing—blossomed, changing the face of America. With every passing day more automobiles could be seen chugging along cobblestone streets and dirt roads. Soon the whole country would be covered with a network of highways and roads, and by their sides would stand garages, filling stations, and roadside diners. Commercial centers would spread out from our inner cities. This decentralization of commerce created an even greater demand for the automobile. The age of the automobile had arrived. It would provide a new path to profits spurring economic growth just as the railroads had some 50 years earlier. This new industry grew at breathtaking speed and generated in its wake a host of supporting and collateral industries, such as oil and tires. Confidence in the future spread.

Confidence that the economic future is brighter usually awakens an idealistic and reforming spirit. People believe the economic and social problems that have plagued mankind for centuries can be quickly and painlessly solved. There is no doubt that some reforms do help, however people feel they have greater control over their destiny than they actually do.

For example, in 1913, in response to the financial panic of 1907, the U.S. created the Federal Reserve Bank to solve the problem of recurring economic boom and bust. The Fed's basic job was to manage the nation's money so we would always have enough to sustain the economy but not so much as to cause inflation. However, as the history of the past eighty years shows, recession and inflation did not disappear. Or for instance, shortly after World War I we adopted prohibition, naively thinking we could change morality and rid society of the abuses and wastes attributed to alcohol. In actuality, prohibition created at least as many problems as it solved.

At about this time in the expansion a major war typically occurs. The great economic strides being made by the innovating nation threaten the world equilibrium. Either an emerging economic power becomes aggressive in its search for resources and markets, or the dominant power feels threatened by a rising new power and attempts to preempt the newcomer by military might. In either case a fight for world dominance is likely to take place at this time in the cycle. In 1917, the United States followed its

friends, Britain and France, into World War I and emerged
as the world's leading power.

However taxing this war seems emotionally, the huge
injections of money into the war effort along with a heightened need for scarce supplies of labor and goods produces
a special buoyancy to the economy. Even the most mar-
ginal and risky ventures prosper. Suddenly it becomes
clear that the borrowers and risk takers have been running away with the profits, while the savers and lenders
have been left with the risk. The shift from risk aversion
to risk taking turns into a stampede. The economy looks
rosier and people come to trust this prosperity. Why not
take some risks, they reason. As the risk takers multiply,
the tempo of business picks up, expectations soar, consumer demand reaches unprecedented levels, and the
long-term rate of interest skyrockets.

Psychology of Affluence

In this atmosphere of ever increasing prosperity, a change
in psychology spreads over the whole of the social fabric.
People feel more powerful and develop the psychology of
affluence. The pleasure principle takes over. People want
to have fun and live the good life. They no longer feel the
need to cooperate for the common good, so individualism
rises again and with it an increase in assertiveness, ego-
tism, and arrogance.

Following our participation in World War I a social revolution took place. There was a rapid change in our mores.
People shook off the restraints of Puritanism and adopted
attitudes radically different from those held at the turn of

the century. A rebellious younger generation went on a rampage of hell-raising. They revolted against discipline and parental authority. They wanted excitement, and the thrill of living for the moment. Thus began the "Jazz Age," featuring hip flasks, flappers, and the Charleston. Hedonism blossomed. The American public discovered Freud and read his message as "repression is bad." Outlandish types of behavior were tolerated. There was a vast increase in the divorce rate; in 1910, 8.8 of every 100 marriages ended in divorce, by 1928, this had increased to 16.5 of every 100. Woman, having just recently gotten the vote, threw off the conventions of the Victorian period and sought to enjoy themselves with the same freedom men did. They began painting their faces with lipstick and rouge, lifted their skirts all the way to the knee, stepped out of their corsets, and began smoking cigarettes and drinking gin in public. The sexual revolution of the 1920s saw "nice" girls engaging in "petting parties" and kissing boys at will. "I've kissed dozens of men, and I suppose I'll kiss dozens more," confessed one of F. Scott Fitzgerald's heroines. There was a proliferation of sex and confession magazines, which were gobbled up by a public obsessed with the subject.

Demands for social change increased and set off an explosion in the level of civil disorder, ending the period of social tranquillity that had accompanied the earlier part of the expansion. Traditional authorities and institutions came under attack. Everyone, it seems, was ready to have a go at "getting theirs."

A wave of increasing crime, violence, and strikes sent a shiver down the spine of the middle class. Following World War I, the Ku Klux Klan spread to the North; a bomb, supposedly set by Bolsheviks or anarchists, exploded on

Wall Street right across from the leading banking firm of
J. P. Morgan & Co., killing 30 people, and a multitude of
unauthorized strikes shut down municipal governments
for days at a time.

The most striking event of the late teens was a raging
inflation. The price of nearly all commodities soared. By
1920 the price of silk rose to the unheard-of level of $18.40
per pound, while wheat, which for years had been changing hands at about $1 a bushel, skyrocketed to $3.50 per
bushel. There was a frenzy of speculative activity on the
stock exchanges. Unlike the inflation that had stimulated
business activity at the beginning of the expansion, this
later inflation was a sign that people's expectations had
become too high. It became more profitable to try to out-
guess the inflation than to engage in productive efforts,
and business people began to speculate in commodities
rather than produce them. Money that normally flowed
into productive channels was now used to finance the
inflation. As a result, it became very difficult to increase
supplies. The relationship between effort and reward was
undermined and the work ethic was dulled, thus leading
to a sharp decline in productivity.

Seeds of Recession

In 1917, long-term interest rates reached 5 percent surpassing the natural rate, which with inflation averaging
about 1 percent during the past decade could be pegged at
approximately 4½ percent. The willingness to pay more
for money than the natural rate of interest indicates that
people were committing an error of optimism. Expectations
in the future of the economy and the desire to be a risk

taker had become too high. With business costs exceeding the ability of business to raise prices, the economy was again overextended, only this time much more seriously than in 1906.

Almost overnight the economy plummeted into serious recession. Amidst a widespread cancellation of retail and industrial orders, a sweeping deflation began. By late 1921 the price of silk dropped to $5.80 per pound and wheat returned to $1 per bushel. The stock market plummeted 47 percent; industrial production fell 30 percent; and unemployment reached the highest levels since the depression of the 1890s. People's confidence was severely shaken and with President Wilson incapacitated by a stroke, many lost faith in the government's ability to handle economic problems.

However, not all profitable investment opportunities had been exploited, and productive facilities had not yet been overbuilt. Also too many people remained committed to an expanding economy to let the deflation run its natural course. Central bankers, big business, and big government all rallied to the rescue of the economy. In 1921, the Federal Reserve flooded the economy with cheap and easy money. Leading corporations came to the aid of their ailing brethren. Du Pont bailed out General Motors, which had accumulated an excessive amount of debt and tottered on the brink of bankruptcy. The system shuddered a bit but stayed intact. A long lasting depression did not set in.

Nonetheless, the heightened economic expectations of the past few years cooled. Life did not appear quite so easy. People became a bit more cautious and a bit less inclined to take on economic risk. As a result, both long-term interest rates and wholesale prices fell, lowering the cost of doing business.

Caution Breeds Conservatism

As the worst did not happen, people regained their confidence, and the economy began expanding. Initially people's optimism was tempered by a new maturity. They were disillusioned with crusades for noble causes and no longer willing to follow anyone who promised a parade to the promised land. Instead, they wanted to enjoy themselves. In a nutshell, the American people became more conservative, both politically and economically.

In 1920 an amiable but undistinguished senator from Ohio, Warren G. Harding, got himself elected President by promising a "return to normalcy." The new administration proposed a program featuring economy in federal expenditures, deregulation, and tax cuts. The wealthy saw their tax burden fall from 50 percent to 20 percent, and the frosting on their cake was the elimination of the wartime excise tax. A tidal wave of prosperity followed. Social tensions eased. Real estate boomed and the stock market thundered from one new high to another. The more promising investment ideas were soon exploited. More and more business people were drawn to the newer and more successful industries and products. The automobile and its supporting industries grew by leaps and bounds. By 1929, there were 23 million passenger automobiles on American roads compared to the 6½ million in 1919; the automobile industry accounted for more than a tenth of the value of all manufactured goods. A recession hit in 1923, but it was mild and the economy quickly recovered.

Once again, in 1927 a recession struck, however it was barely noticeable.

To most observers the Roaring '20s was a triumphant decade of economic progress. However, beneath the surface there were cracks and fissures. The price level which had begun falling in 1920 kept sinking, which created much hardship for the nation's farmers. They faced adversity throughout much of the decade. Productivity sagged. Certain industries, such as coal mining and textiles, and certain regions such as the South and Northwest, were being left behind in the dash for riches, as were the European economies, especially Britain. Intensifying competition made it difficult for business firms to raise prices and profit margins began to erode. The deepest fissure—tremendous debt—developed because the optimism of the time had seduced businesses people and consumers. People had borrowed to build plants or businesses; they had borrowed to buy stocks; and they had borrowed to increase their standard of living. For instance, in order to move the mass of new consumer products, businesses created installment buying. Consumers took the bait and began hocking future paychecks so they could have the latest new gadget or appliance now. Soon it was thought old fashioned to limit purchases to the amount of one's cash balance. Furthermore, according to the Brookings Institute, "there [had] been a tendency . . . for the inequality in the distribution of income to be accentuated." Despite people's confidence in the economy, the '20s were, in fact, a period of uneven economic growth.

The period of 1927 to 1929 was one of excessive optimism. In late 1927 Charles Lindbergh captured the imagination of the masses by flying the Atlantic Ocean nonstop. "The greatest feat of a solitary man in the records of the human race" breathlessly claimed the *New York Evening World*. There was no doubt that the revolution in transportation was shrinking our world. Once again, business leaders and workers began throwing caution to the winds. Economic commitments were pushed too far and stretched too thin. Herbert Hoover campaigned for the presidency promising the final triumph over poverty. An orgy of speculation unlike anything seen before or since hit our stock exchanges. The public's appetite for common stocks had been whetted by year after year of rising earnings and by Edgar Lawrence Smith's tremendously popular book, *Common Stocks as Long Term Investments*. Up until the publication of this book in 1924, bonds had been thought to be a superior investment to stocks. However, the book demonstrated that in every period during the last 50 years common stocks had out-performed bonds significantly. Soon brokerage offices were jammed with crowds of people, including shoeshine boys, seamstresses, and chauffeurs, willing to pay almost any price to participate in the bull market. *The Ladies' Home Journal* published an article entitled "Everybody Ought To Be Rich," written by one of the most respected business leaders in the country, John Raskob, chief financial officer of General Motors. He claimed, "the way to wealth, is to get into the profit end of wealth production . . .".

Speculative Fever Spreads

The floor of the New York Stock Exchange was filled with "pool operators" controlling large pools of investment dollars. These savvy market professionals sought to push up and manipulate the prices of stocks. In the 18-month period from March 3, 1928, to September 3, 1929, the Dow Jones Industrial Average rose from 191 to 381. Not to mention certain key stocks which were far outperforming the averages; Montgomery Ward went from $133 to $466; Westinghouse from $92 to $313, and RCA, the darling of this bull market, from $95 to $505.[1]

Nor was this speculative fever confined to investors in the stock market. Economists, who we would like to think know better, were also victims of this speculative fever. Because the performance of the economy kept exceeding their forecasts, they thought something new and important must be happening to the economy. According to professor Charles Dice, "a mighty revolution in industry and, in trade, and in finance . . . is taking place." The spreading euphoria also clouded the judgment of the nation's business managers. They actively pursued marginally profitable ventures and piled on layer upon layer of debt. More and more risk takers appeared on the scene, and with them came a proliferation of imitators, financial manipulators, and get-rich-quick schemers all seeking easy fortunes. Naturally, the quality of bank loans deteriorated. and once again the economy became overextended.

This time the overextension was a serious matter. The serious contraction of 1920 had not gone far enough in correcting the problems that had built up during the earlier part of the expansion. Although long-term interest rates had fallen, they still remained well above the natural rate of interest. Labor productivity had improved, but not to the level existing earlier in the expansionary period. Finally, economic expectations, while cooled, were still

---

1   Prices adjusted for stock splits.

high by past standards. Only the grossest excesses had been liquidated.

Thus, the 1920s, while prosperous, had been built on a foundation of sand. They began with a high cost of capital, low labor productivity and a large appetite for risk taking compared to what existed in 1897. New investment had been undertaken at a high level of fixed cost and this put corporate profitability in jeopardy. Businesses continued to pile on high-cost debt to build more productive facilities at the very time competition between business firms and nations was most cutthroat. The economy became vulnerable to a major collapse.

Prosperity Cracks Open

In late 1929 the economy weakened. When investors realized the situation, the speculative bubble burst. Waves of selling hit the nation's stock exchanges and within a ten-week period the Dow Jones Industrial Average shed a chilling 50 percent of its entire 33-year advance and wiped out an estimated one million people who owned stocks on margin. The structure of American prosperity cracked wide open. To no avail, monetary authorities pushed interest rates to the floor. Confidence had been undermined. All the problems that had been pushed under the rug began popping out. Too many bad debts provoked a banking crisis which wiped out the savings of millions of people. The contraction snowballed into a bona fide depression of such terrifying proportions that millions of people would lose faith in capitalism.

The depressionary phase of the cycle began with the depression of 1929-1933. This business contraction, unlike the one in 1920-1921, which was merely a crisis of confidence, provoked a massive loss of confidence. The hopes and illusions of those who had believed in the prosperity were shattered. Long-term interest rates and wholesale prices plummeted. Unemployment reached 25 percent of the work force, business earnings evaporated, bankruptcies abounded, and the output of goods and services was cut in half. The masses of people who had experienced decades of expansion in the value of their capital assets were faced with a catastrophic fall in the value of their assets. Nothing survived the massive downward readjustment in value—not common stocks, not real estate, not antiques, not art. The Dow Jones Industrial Average fell a mind boggling 89 percent from it's 1929 high. Westinghouse sank to $16, RCA to $13, and Montgomery Ward continued on a bumpy downhill slide until it reached a price of $4 a share.

The arrogance and overconfidence of this age were washed away. As the various nations' domestic economies collapsed, they became less willing to make the accommodations necessary to maintain the international monetary and trade system. The international system broke down and the depression became worldwide.

Blaming the depth of the Great Depression on a special event, such as Britain's going off the gold standard in 1931, as many people do, puts the cart before the horse. During times such as those described above, things people did not bargain for come to light. Over 100 years ago, Walter Bagehot, England's leading financial chronicler wrote: "Every great crisis reveals the excessive speculation of many houses which no one before suspected."

The deepening depression shattered people's assumption of a relatively risk-free world. People became more cautious. Hedonistic behavior subsided and there was less tolerance for deviant social behavior. The music slowed. Women lengthened their skirts, dressed more conservatively, began to wear white gloves, and became respectful of a meal ticket. People no longer flagrantly flaunted the sexual code. There was much less ado about sex, while courting and romance came back into their own. Marriage became more highly prized as a social institution and the divorce rate fell. People stayed home and spent more time with their families. Games such as Monopoly and contract bridge became immensely popular.

However, though the frivolousness and open sensuality of the 1920s disappeared, the U. S. did not turn back completely to the old conventions that had existed at the turn of the century. Much of the outlandish behavior was no longer accepted, but many of the new freedoms won by the flappers of the younger generation remained. Women did not retreat to the home; they still held jobs, drank alcohol, and smoked in public.

Capitalism Shunned

A hostility toward capitalism and free markets was born during this depression. A feeling that something had gone terribly wrong with individualistic capitalism spread across the country. Traditional economic laws had not worked. Competition between individuals and firms had proven to be unexpectedly cruel. Competition had brought out the worst in people. The inquiries into the economy that occurred during the depression laid bare the evidence of many unsavory incidents. Respected business leaders were shown to have been dipping into the till, and abuses on the stock exchange were brought to light. In 1932 more than a million Americans voted against the capitalist system, and many younger people dallied with and, in some cases, embraced communism.

Generally, the political party in power at the beginning of a depressionary period is held responsible and kicked out of office. The sharp and prolonged downturn in the economy serves as convincing evidence that those in power are unable to control economic events. In 1932 the Democrats defeated Herbert Hoover and began a long period as the dominant political party. With Franklin Delano Roosevelt at the helm, the Democrats brushed aside the basic doctrines of laissez-faire economics and legislated many reforms to help individuals counteract the harshness of the depression. They became the new majority party and for the next 50 years the Republicans would not hold the White House for more than eight consecutive years.

The new Administration took office and pushed an agenda of relentless reform. A New Deal was proclaimed and the government passed legislation to create Social Security, unemployment insurance, and public works projects. In general, the new administration attempted to create a more equitable and compassionate society. This agenda helped revive some measure of confidence and raised hopes that the economy had seen bottom. Stock and commodity prices experienced a sharp rebound from their depression lows, business earnings increased, and a broad recovery appeared to be in progress.

As this business expansion continued, hopes rose that the economy would return to the heights achieved in late 1920s. However, the liquidation of 1929-1933, while severe, was not complete. We had not completely liquidated excess capacity. Debt liquidation had not run its full course, and business costs while lower, were not dramatically lower. As a result, the recovery was sluggish and unemployment stayed stubbornly high. When business people attempted to pick up the pace by rebuilding inventories and expanding capital expenditures, it was too much for the economy to handle. Another contraction began, and set off a second wave of liquidation, dashing hopes for an early recovery and return to prosperity.

The Heart of the Depression

While not so severe as the preceding one, this second contraction was also of major proportions. The dominant industry, the automobile, was hit with an epidemic of bankruptcies and as the weaker companies were weeded out, excess capacity was brought down. The railroads, which by now had out served their usefulness, were in very serious trouble. Again, prices of stocks and commodities broke sharply. The expectation that we would recover from this economic debacle was jolted. There was a stampede to become risk averters. The long-term rate of interest fell below the natural rate, signalling that people were committing an error of pessimism. The period from 1929 through the second depression, which ended in 1938, was the heart of the depressionary phase.

As the depression lengthened, disillusionment deepened. The change in mood became even more striking. The prolonged slump had undermined the financial assets, job security, career objectives, and the ability to cope financially. People felt helpless and lost faith in their own powers. Their notion of risk changed. The dominant goal was to avoid pain, creating a psychology of deflation. The focus shifted toward protecting oneself against what might lie ahead. People became more accommodating and cooperative, more trusting and more willing to accept protective authority that would provide some direction. A sense of community and camaraderie took hold. The younger generation became more respectful of their parents and less scornful of the older traditional values. In the economic sphere people grew more cautious and much less inclined to take a risk. They valued security, seeking safe, unadventurous jobs. People began saving for the future.

The widespread misery and discontent during these times of course produces a great deal of social unrest. However, it is unlike the social strife during prosperous periods. This time the enemy is clear-cut and more basic. It is the depression. No other problem seems so vital or pressing. People band together, demanding protection from the harshness of an impersonal economy. For example, in the 1930s there were many particularly bloody mass-organizing strikes by the Congress of Industrial Organizations (CIO), and in 1932, an army of 15,000 unemployed veterans of World War I marched on Washington hoping to persuade Congress to distribute the bonus certificates that had already been promised.

The depression of the 1930s was so terrifying and so prolonged that it provoked a search for its cause and a strong desire to ensure it would never happen again. We soon focused on the British economist, John Maynard Keynes's diagnosis of insufficient demand. Keynes observed that once confidence in the economy was destroyed, spending could fall to a level which was insufficient to soak up the supply of goods, and an economy could wallow in this state of affairs for a disturbingly long period of time. He recommended that when this happened the government should step into the breach and inject purchasing power into the economy. In 1946, the Full Employment Act was passed. The government assumed responsibility to support demand and maintain full employment. A patchwork of legislation designed to prop up the economy and rig the marketplace in favor of the underdog was enacted. Competition was curbed in order to protect business firms. The nature of the American economy was permanently altered. Laissez-faire capitalism was dismantled and in its place was a new Keynesian economic order, wherein the government was responsible for maintaining the health of the economy.

By the earlier 1940s much of the debt and excess capacity had been liquidated and a business recovery began. However, following the last recovery hopes were shattered and widespread disillusionment had set in. People did not believe that real improvement was developing in many sectors of the economy. They thought it was largely a consequence of World War II and kept looking over their shoulders for a recurrence of the depression. As a result, stock prices and interest rates, did not reflect the real improvement in business. Because of the prevailing apprehension, in 1945, when it became apparent that peace was at hand, people reduced their spending and we got another contraction followed by a sharp stock market break.

This contraction again shattered the emerging confidence and cast a pall over business, which kept the subsequent recovery brief, and in 1948 we got yet another recession. However, these two contractions were less severe than the preceding ones. As people started to recognize the improvement in business conditions, they began to loosen their purse strings. As business costs had been reduced, the cost of capital became cheap and the return of the work ethic brought about a dramatic improvement in labor productivity. New investment could now be undertaken at a low level of fixed cost.

By 1949, one complete cycle had ended and we were ready to begin another long period of prosperity. But before I discuss the next long cycle, let me digress and show that this long cycle of boom and bust had occurred over and over again before the nineteenth century.

NINETEENTH CENTURY ENGLAND
• • • • • •

The same experience of a long period of prosperity followed by a period of depression also occurred in England during the nineteenth century. Britain's example can be especially useful to us because during the 19th century England was the major source of finance and advanced technology, just as the United States is today.

Following the outbreak of industrialism in the late eighteenth century, Great Britain experienced two long cycles that appear strikingly similar to the cycle of 1897-1949 in the United States.

Chapter Three

In the mid 1780s inflation imported from France, England's chief trading partner, stimulated industrial activity in Britain and lifted the economy off the runway. The first long cycle had begun and the driving force for what was to be the first phase of industrialization was the steam engine which James Watt had perfected about fifteen years earlier. The substitution of power-driven machines for work formerly done by hundreds of horses or men stimulated a massive increase in industrial output. And nowhere was the application of steam power more noticeable than in the flourishing textile industry. The rapid spread of cotton mills throughout the nation provided the innovational impetus for the expansion, just as the automobile was to do for the U.S. expansion of 1897-1929. Cotton was the first mass-produced consumer good, and soon it would change the habits and dress of whole nations.

During this expansion Britain was drawn into a bitter war with France to quell Napoleon's grandiose ambition. As world leadership hung in the balance, neither side was prepared to settle for less than total victory. This was a no-holds-barred war, much more so than any in the past 100 years, and it set off a rampaging inflation in England, and precipitated a surge in the long term-rate of interest. This was the sign that too many demands were being placed on the economy.

There was also a great deal of social unrest at that time. Groups of workers called, Luddites, went on a rampage destroying the new machines that had been taking away jobs. The first shot in what was to be a centuries long war for women's equality was fired with the publication, in 1792, of Mary Wollstonecraft's, "Vindication of the Rights of Woman," a treatise that called for equal rights and equal opportunities for all human beings irrespective of their sex. However, there was little reaction to it at the time.

Following Napoleon's defeat, Britain was the recognized leader of the world. There was a very serious business contraction in 1815, which cast a pall over the economy for the next three years. This, of course, cooled overheated expectations. Soon the pace of industrialization intensified. Entrepreneurs accumulated and reinvested capital on a truly awesome scale. New applications of steam power were found and applied to more and more products. A tidal wave of prosperity produced a euphoria in the British people as to their economic prospects, quite similar to that which the American people were to experience following World War I. A great wave of speculation hit the stock exchange, and the leading industries of cotton, coal, and iron experienced unprecedented expansion which, of course, led to vast overproduction.

Capitalism Called into Question

In 1825, a financial crisis struck and ushered in a period of depression that was so extraordinary men were at a loss for a precedent. Industrial activity ground to a halt, unemployment rose to exceedingly high levels, and many businessmen faced ruin. The price of assets collapsed. By one estimate, stock prices fell by over 80 percent. Real income per head, the basic tenet of economic progress, actually fell in the 1830s for the first time since the early 1700s. People were reduced to a degree of squalor and misery never subsequently paralleled in Britain and this produced labor unrest on a frightening scale. This period was the most politically and socially disruptive in Britain's

history. In fact, it was the first crisis in industrial capitalism, and there was much doubt about whether this new
system of economic affairs would survive.

In response to an angry and frustrated people, there was
a political realignment. The Whig, or Liberal, party attained political dominance, which it would hang onto for
fifty years, and put forward a program of reform which was
to transform the structure of society to conform to the
great economic and social changes of the late eighteenth
and early nineteenth centuries. The Reform Act of 1832,
gave most middle class men the right to vote and laid the
foundation of modern democracy. This parliamentary reform was the first step to other changes, which soon followed. The grievances of the working class, who were
shortchanged during the immense buildup of wealth that
had taken place during the prior upswing, were redressed.
A striking series of humanitarian reforms such as legislation mandating minimum working conditions for women
and children, was passed. This was intriguingly similar to
what was to happen in the U. S. a century later.

A spate of legislation based on the ideas of Adam Smith
came next. Smith and his followers felt that businessmen,
if left alone from government interference, would, in their
desire for profits, act in such a way as to secure prosperity.
Government policy was aimed at removing regulations
and restraints on trade and establishing the marketplace
as the basic arbiter of economic affairs. Workers were
thrown out of the workhouse so that labor would also become
a commodity to be bought and sold in the marketplace.
Duties were removed or reduced on hundreds of items.
Finally and most importantly, the Corn Laws were re-
pealed, removing duties on food, and free trade became a

reality. Great Britain was transformed into a laissez-faire, capitalistic society that furnished a model for other nations to follow. By the late 1840s Britain's first cycle of expansion and depression was complete.

Victorian Boom Brings Prosperity

In about 1848 the Great Victorian boom began. This was a period of golden prosperity very similar to what the American people were to experience following World War II. It began when new gold discoveries in California and Australia set off an inflation that stimulated business activity. The boom was spurred on by the development of the railroad. This was to be the first phase in a revolution of transportation that would endure and provide the thrust for industrialization for the next hundred years. As prosperity took hold and spread, the value of assets began a 30-year climb.

The early years of this prosperity, until the 1860s, were a time of social tranquillity. The railroad, by its gargantuan appetite for iron and coal, stimulated the expansion of other industries and opened up new sources of food and raw materials. Above all, the railroad speeded up transport and reduced its cost. The movement of people became far easier, traveling now coming within the reach of all but the very poorest of the working class. Industrial activity, world trade, and employment grew by leaps and bounds. The trickle of mass-produced goods became a torrent, and middle and working class families experienced a massive increase in their living standards. The world had never before seen such a rapid and sustained increase in wealth and prosperity. Rapid progress in health and longevity was achieved. And during this period, international conflicts did not get out of hand as had happened 50 years earlier because no country achieved the economic strength to pose an important threat to British hegemony. England was not drawn in to a major war during this cycle.

However, across the Atlantic ocean, the American South, which was economically and politically tied to England by virtue of producing seven-eighths of the world's cotton, became involved in a major conflict. The Civil War, like most wars occurring at this point in the cycle, was very inflationary, and provided a major stimulus to the British economy, as lost markets had to be replaced and Confederate capital sought refuge there. This provided the stimulus to heighten England's expectations, and a frenzy of speculative activity soon followed. The long-term rate of interest spiked up just as it had 50 years earlier, signaling that people's expectations had become too high.

Bank's Support Cools Down Recession

The economy became temporarily overextended, and in 1866 Britain suffered a serious recession wherein confidence was severely shaken. It began on May 11, 1866, Black Friday in England, as Overend Gurney and Company, one of the leading banking houses of that time, failed. According to the *London Times,* the shock could be felt in the "remotest corners of the Kingdom" and "panic...swayed the City to and fro." The government came to the economy's aid by suspending the Bank Charter Act, so that the Bank of England could provide support to the business community. As a result, this contraction did not worsen. Expectations were cooled, confidence was restored, and soon there was a resurgence of economic vitality, similar to what occurred in the United States following the serious contraction of 1920-1921.

The social tranquillity ended in the mid 1860s. Darwin's just-published theory of evolution, which held that man had descended from the apes, shocked middle class society. The notion that man had been made in God's image was challenged and this began to break the hold of religion as a living force. During the following 100 years we would experience a revolt against the traditional values associated with religion, as a wild search for earthly happiness picked up steam. A new set of values based on living for today and for personal gratification, such as hedonism, consumption, and leisure, would become the norm.

The first real round of feminism began shortly after the appearance of John Stuart Mill's work "The Subjection of Women" in 1869. Women were soon displaying a degree of self-assertiveness most unusual for the time, stepping out of the home and embarking on a wide range of new careers, from nursing to school teaching to secretarial and sales work, all of which were newly opened to them.

Most people attributed the astonishing growth of business to Britain's practice of free enterprise, just as the Americans a century later were to attribute their prosperity to Keynesian economics. Free trade became the basic economic tenet of the ordinary Britisher's liberal creed. The great economists elaborated on Adam Smith's ideas, and the politicians swept the statute books clear of the remaining interferences in the marketplace. Mid-Victorian Britain came as near to being a laissez-faire capitalistic economy as had ever been possible in modern times. Conservatives today look back on this period with nostalgia.

Just as Lindbergh's nonstop flight over the Atlantic had captured the imagination of the masses, so too did the opening of the Suez Canal in 1869. The year 1869 also marked the completion of the first American transcontinental railroad, an accomplishment that inspired worldwide confidence. In the following four years, there was furious industrial activity and a frenetic pace of railroad building. Twenty-four thousand miles of railroad were built in the United States alone, much of it financed by British capital. Much of this credit was extended loosely and without proper regard for the economic and financial soundness of the venture.

When coal, the main agent of industry, soared over 125 percent there was much concern that Britain's coal reserves were being exhausted and this would end the spread of steam power to new industries. Finally, the newly industrialized nations of Germany and the United States were flooding British markets, which because of free trade were unprotected, with an outpouring of cheap goods. Yet, in spite of these problems business conditions appeared sound.

Britain Rides Crest before Fall

By the early 1870s, Britain's phenomenal success was visible to all. She possessed two-thirds of the world's cotton factory production, accounted for one-half of the world's output of iron and coal, and truly was the Workshop of the

World. The British people, who were riding the crest of a twenty-five-year boom the likes of which the world had never seen, felt a sense of progress, well-being, and achievement. Certainly they thought nothing very serious was likely to go wrong.

But, in 1873, the British economy, along with the rest of the industrial world, sunk into another long slump. In the following 12 years there was but one feeble business recovery which soon vanished into thin air. Each time the troubles appeared to be passing, additional defaults or other problems struck, and the skies became overcast again. And during this whole period, prices, profits, and interest rates stayed puzzlingly low. Businessmen were harassed by severe competition, falling profit margins, and in the capital goods industries, much excess capacity. For example, it was reported that in the late 1870s worldwide capacity to produce steel rails was almost two and a half million tons, while annual consumption was only running at about 500,000 to 600,000 tons.

In British history books the period 1873-1897 is generally referred to as "the Great Depression." The continuing drop in prices along with intensified competition from the German and United States economies made it very difficult for merchants to survive, let alone make a profit. Business people at all levels complained of the "commercial paralysis" and "the deplorable state of the trade." The basic industries, such as shipbuilding and iron molding were in deep trouble similar to that which plagues the auto, steel and construction industries today. Thirty-four percent of the shipbuilders were out of work, while unemployment in the iron molding industry reached 22 percent—truly awesome figures.

Chapter Three

The enthusiasm of the earlier period gave way to doubt and disenchantment. There was a general reaction against the harsh and impersonal laws of the marketplace which had been revealed during the slump. The boundaries of state activity were extended to ensure the welfare of the people. And business increasingly sought safety, as in earlier times, in regulation and agreement. Laissez-faire capitalism was modified, though by no means was it abandoned. The structure of society and the economy was not transformed as it had been during the depression of the 1830s. This was because the depression was not severe enough to frighten the British people to undertake sweeping change. Although the prices of stocks, bonds, and land plummeted, the economy did not experience the spectacular breakdown it had in the 1830s.

British Stubbornly Cling to Free Trade

British businesses felt threatened by the stiff competition the newer more energetic economies of Germany and the U.S. were offering. Free trade, which had been imposed on the economy during the last depression, had come back to haunt the British, much as Keynesian economics and its seductive appeal to budget deficits haunts the U.S. today. The loss of Britain's ability to compete successfully for export markets was thought to be the culprit of this depression. Lord Randolph Churchill sponsored a "Fair Trade League" which was the first serious challenge to the idea of free trade. However, even though the rest of the developed world abandoned free trade, Britain stubbornly clung to this sacred doctrine. Instead, she sought to extend her market by pursuing an aggressive policy of imperialism which would allow her to dominate some of the backward markets of the world. This enabled her to conceal the fact that she was a power in decline for a while longer.

There was also a great deal of social strife, including serious rioting in London during this time as the trade unions fought bitterly and blindly to protect the jobs and living standards of its members. Gloom and doomers, warning of an apocalyptic economic collapse, began to appear in all the major cities. The most famous of those 19th century prophets of disaster was Karl Marx, who was, of course, predicting the final collapse of capitalism. The dominance of the Liberal Party was broken at this time, and new reforms were put in place, which focused on unions and factory safety, or protecting the individual.

To be sure, some contemporary economists, after having reconstructed the statistics, wonder what the big fuss was all about. They note that the newer consumer industries and the southern areas of the country held up quite well. Furthermore because wages did not fall as rapidly as prices, and except for the worst years unemployment remained below ten percent, the working class actually found themselves better off. The British economist, S.B. Saul, who studied this period, stated, "The sooner the (term) 'Great Depression' is banished from the literature, the better."

The confusion as to whether or not there was a real depression results because the liquidation of unsound enterprise was spaced out in such a way as to avoid the spectacular collapse that we were to experience in the 1930s. However if by depression we mean that the poor performance of the economy has induced a state of mind of unrelieved gloom, there is no question that England experienced a depression during those years. The sense of despair and loss of hope that the economy would ever get much better resembled the mood and attitude in the U.S. during the 1930s. It was the time according to most historians of the 19th century, wherein the British people lost their Victorian sense of courage and optimism.

To the middle class it was certainly a period of hard times. Huge drops in the stock market and real estate to levels not seen since the 1830s, along with extraordinary large defaults on bonds were a crushing blow. Carriages, the chief symbol of nineteenth century affluence, were laid up in record numbers for the first time in four decades. In fact, the agitation of the middle class reached such an urgency that a Royal Commission was set up to look into the causes of the depression.

Technical Edge Lost

This period of hard times lasted until about 1897. During this time Britain was reluctant to fully adopt the new power source of electric power. She was committed to the energy and technology of the past phase of industrialization and did not want to tear up her industrial base and begin anew. Once the next cycle began, it would become apparent that Great Britain had lost her technological edge.

Up until 1949 there had been three long periods of expansion, each of which was generally recognized as a time of widespread and growing prosperity. In each case a seminal technological innovation launched an important new industry which was deployed throughout the economy in the period of about a generation. The rapid development of this new industry spilled over into other areas of the economy and produced extraordinary growth and enormous increases of living standards. Each Kondratieff upswing was accompanied by an important mood shift. People adopted an incredible optimism and began to act in a way that was not economically justified.

The most important similarity of Kondratieff up waves was the long secular rise in the long-term interest rate (see Figure 3–1). In each case it continued until it exceeded the natural rate of interest. This was the sign that people were committing an error of optimism and the groundwork was being laid for a period of retrenchment. Following the break in these long-term interest rates during a serious contraction, interest rates stabilized at a level not far below their peaks. Thus, during the remainder of the expansion, the cost of new investment remained relatively high, putting a crimp in business profits and within a relatively short period of time, depression followed.

During this same time span we had three long waves of economic hardship, high levels of unemployment and falling values of financial assets. By any account of the time

Table 3–1

Expansionary Phase	Depressionary Phase	Peak Expectations	Heart of Depressionary Period
England			
1780s-1825	1825-1848	1814	1825-32
1848-1873	1873-1897	1866	1873-85
United States			
1897-1929	1929-1949	1920	1929-38
1949-1990		1980	

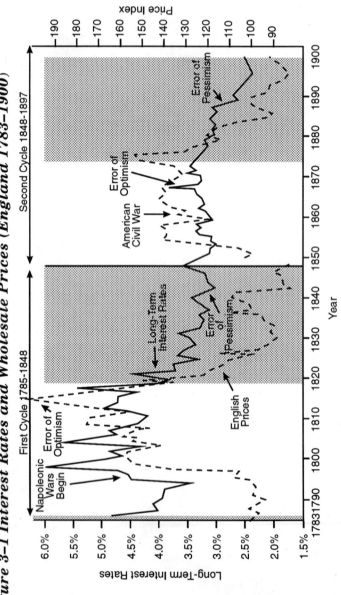

Figure 3-1 Interest Rates and Wholesale Prices (England 1783–1900)

First Cycle 1785-1848

Second Cycle 1848-1897

Depressionary Periods

Note: Shaded areas represent depressionary periods. PriceIndexes, Clough 1783–1900; Sauerbeck Wholesale price index 1850–1900.

Sources: A History of Interest Rates, Second Edition by Sidney Homer, 1963, 1977 by Rutgers, The State University of NJ. Reprinted by permission of Rutgers University Press; "Economic History of Europe" by Clough & Cole.

there was a profound change in the mood of the people to one of gloom and despair. Each time it appeared that the death knell of capitalism had tolled. Just as a period of economic prosperity brings with it the belief that the economy is risk free, a prolonged period of economic distress produces a sense of despair and a loss of faith in capitalism. People feel helpless and lose faith in their own powers. There is a search for the culprit and an attempt at widespread reform. Finally, as the great majority of people became risk averters, the excess capacity developed during the prior expansion is worked off, and there is a dramatic fall in business costs at the very time a pent-up demand is developing. This, of course, lays the groundwork for a return to good times. The pain and suffering we feel during these periods of economic distress are not the death throes of industrialization, but rather, the birth pangs of a new prosperity.

It was only during the depressionary periods, when confidence was lost, that the stock market was able to fall more than 50 percent from its highs. This drop occurred three times since we have kept records: first in the 1870s, then in 1929-1933, and finally, from 1937 to 1942. But the most significant similarity and undeniable sign of bad times was the decline in long-term interest rates, lasting throughout the depressionary period, to well below the natural rate of interest, signaling that the vast majority of people were committing an error of pessimism.

By 1949, we had three complete cycles of economic activity, from bust to boom to bust again. Does the post-World War II period follow this underlying rhythm or are things different this time? That is the subject of the next chapter.

THE PRESENT CYCLE
● ● ● ● ● ●

In 1949, the United States economy emerged from a 20-year depression and began what would be a decades-long period of almost uninterrupted prosperity. The financing of two wars, World War II and Korea, led to an inflation which, in turn, set the forces of expansion in motion. There was a burst of economic energy, consumer demand exploded, and industry expanded to meet the demand. The automobile industry, the dominant industry of the last cycle, revived. The stock market started a long advance, and long-term interest rates began what was to be a 32-year rise (see Figure 2–1).

Chapter Four

The 1950s were a period of social tranquillity much like the one that had occurred at the beginning of the century. The conservative, more traditional values and life styles fashioned during the depression, remained throughout the beginning of the following upswing. The stimulative inflation was easily cooled and the following two recessions were relatively mild. In retrospect, they were dull but good years, wherein the American people were pleased with the way things were going. The United States was indisputably the top nation. America had a currency that was the world's standard, a productive capacity that was unrivaled, export markets that took everything she produced and begged for more.

By 1959 confidence in the economy was beginning to spread. A wave of speculative activity, directed mostly into new issues, hit the stock exchanges. Businesses stepped up their spending, and the cost of capital rose sharply. Business had become temporarily overextended.

The result was the business recession of 1960-1961. Although this recession was milder than the one of 1958 in terms of unemployment or falloff in industrial activity, it had a bigger impact on the psychological indicators, interest rates and stock prices. The broad rise in long-term interest rates was interrupted by a three-year decline. In 1962, when President Kennedy attempted to roll back steel prices, just as American business firms were emerging from the recession, the stock market suffered its biggest decline in 25 years. The result was that this recession, along with the sharp stock market break that followed, served to shake the nation's emerging confidence, just as the serious recession of 1907 had 55 years earlier.

However, the underlying business conditions were sound, and the economy did not turn down into depression. Once people got the message to proceed more cautiously, speculative activity and some of the excesses disappeared; the government passed the Investment Tax Credit Act, proposed an income tax cut, and there was a resurgence of economic vitality.

Computer Age Dawns

We recovered from this recession, to discover the revolution in transportation which had severed as the energizing force of industrialization for the past 100 years had spent its force. However, waiting in the wings and ready to play its role was a radical new way in which we were to use knowledge. At its center was another seminal innovation, the computer, which like the railroad of the 19th century, was allowing businesses to substitute capital for labor and organize on a much larger, more efficient scale. The following years saw a sweeping change in the way of doing business and an ever-expanding market for computers as banks, hospitals, brokerage firms, merchandisers, and others quickly computerized their operations. The age of the automobile gave way to the age of the computer, which provided a new path to profits.

As the boom rolled on, the strength of the U. S. economy seemed inexhaustible. Middle and working class families found themselves awash in a flood of consumer goods and were becoming accustomed to the idea that every year would see an improvement in living standards. The value of financial assets climbed, business owners increased their capital expenditures, and long-term interest rates resumed their upward march.

On November 22, 1963 an assassin's bullet shattered the tranquillity that had characterized the 1950s and early '60s and America began what appears to be the most revolutionary decade in its history thus far. Lyndon Johnson assumed the presidency and a tidal wave of social and economic legislation was passed, with the belief we could cure all the miseries of the human condition and at the same time build a "Great Society." War was waged against poverty and racial injustice.

By the late 1960s we thought Keynesian economics was responsible for our extraordinary success, much like the British a century earlier, attributed their good fortune to the imposition of free trade. Politicians of nearly every stripe fell into line. In 1971 Richard Nixon, a Republican president, emphatically stated, "We are all Keynesians now." Keynesian economics had worked remarkably well. The period following World War II had been the most prosperous the world had ever seen. Recessions were brief, mild, and infrequent. Each time the economy went into a stall, the government turned up its engine, increased its spending, and shortly thereafter the economy righted itself and roared back to new high levels.

We finished the job of building Keynesian safeguards into the economy and people thought we had achieved a limitless ever-growing prosperity. George Stigler, conservative president of the American Economic Association, declared his profession had developed all the major concepts and theories needed to ensure stable prices and full employment.

Vietnam War Boosts Economy

With a crusading spirit that we would stop the spread of Communism, the U.S. entered into Vietnam, an emotional and taxing war. The consequent war effort sent the economy skyrocketing. Expectations soared. Real estate prices took off and the stock market became a scene of frantic speculative activity unlike anything seen since 1929. Egged on by a University of Chicago study that showed the rate of return in the stock market at 9 percent per annum compounded, which was far greater than most alternative investments, stock prices soared. Institutional investors were abandoning their traditional long-term goals and instead emphasizing yearly, and then quarterly performance. The resulting increase in volume was so huge, the back offices of brokerage firms could not keep up with the necessary paperwork. Small private companies were being bought out at ridiculously high prices and scores of new multimillionaires were being created daily. Moreover long-term interest rates reached 5½ percent exceeding the natural rate of interest, which was adjusted for an assumed 2 percent inflation rate. This, of course, was the signal that people were committing an error of optimism, just as they had 50 years earlier.

There was an attitudinal change, much like the one that followed World War I, based on a world that appeared less risky and this spread throughout the social and political fabric. People, once again, developed a psychology of affluence wherein the dominant theme in their behavior became the pursuit of pleasure. A rapid change in society's manners and morals followed. It was to be the dawn of the Age of Aquarius, a time when people would be less interested in achieving success and more intent on "doing their own thing," when short skirted woman would become independent, take the "pill," and partake in the same sexual freedom long enjoyed by men, when the human spirit would liberate itself from the discipline and authority of repressive social and political institutions.

In actuality, it was a period of increasing hedonism, acid rock, mind-expanding drugs, hippie communes, and instant gratification. The music became louder and sexual mores loosened. This time the sexual revolution went way beyond "kissing dozens of men." It was okay now to have sex before marriage—perhaps with dozens of men. The moral moorings of earlier generations were severed. The idea that we could be liberated from those economic chains which in the past had kept us from achieving personal fulfillment once again got a ready response. A generation gap cracked opened along with a challenge to authority which rocked the very institutions on which our social system rests. Feminism reemerged, although this time in a more robust form than fifty years earlier.

Demands for social change increased. The countries college campuses were in turmoil. Black ghettoes in more than a hundred cities—from Los Angeles to Detroit—exploded with a wave of crime, lawlessness, and terror. Extreme political groups, such as the Weathermen and the Black Panthers, had the middle class quacking in their Gucci boots. Bombings, skyjackings, and other forms of terrorism became an almost daily occurrence.

Following a relatively mild recession in 1970, a surge in consumer demand set prices climbing. In late 1971 president Richard Nixon closed the gold window and broke up the Bretton Woods world monetary system—and inflation took off. The price of copper went from $.50 to $1.50 per pound, soybeans from $3.50 to $12.90 per bushel, and sugar, starting at 5 cents, hit the unheard of price of 66 cents per pound. Americans were paying 60 cents for a loaf of bread, which could have been purchased two years earlier for just 27 cents. Again it had become easier to make money betting on price moves, and capital was drawn away from productive economic functions in order to finance speculative ventures. The work ethic dulled and labor turnover, absenteeism, and strikes increased sharply. The resulting high costs impeded business profitability.

OPEC Precipitates Crisis

During the long boom the world economies had developed a voracious appetite for oil, the oxygen of industrial life. Consumption was growing faster than new reserves could be found. In late 1973 a thunderbolt struck the economy. OPEC, an organization of the major oil producing nations, cut the production and drove up the price of oil to unimagined heights. Block-long gasoline lines formed. This was the signal that the world was entering a period of tightening energy supplies. The U.S. could no longer be certain of enough fuel to keep its factories running and homes heated.

The economy tumbled into deep recession and on Wall Street stocks suffered their worst break in 35 years. Moreover, Watergate surfaced to impede whatever ability the current administration might have had to deal with the inflation, and this shook confidence much more seriously than in 1962. Unemployment rose to the highest levels since the last depression and a deflation set in. The price of most commodities came tumbling down. By 1975 copper was down to $.50 a pound, soybeans sold at $4.50, and sugar was bumping along the bottom at 8 cents a pound. Things looked pretty bleak for a while. However, just as they did in 1921, the leaders came to the aid of the economy. Taxes were cut, foreign loans were hastily arranged. New York City, which was on the verge of bankruptcy, was bailed out. With life again appearing not quite so easy, expectations fell, savings increased, and long-term interest rates broke, lowering business costs somewhat. As the profitable investment opportunities had not been fully exploited nor the productive facilities overbuilt, we were able to patch the economy before a depression set in.

Business revived and people started to regain confidence. The stock market turned up. Americans became a bit more conservative and less concerned about grand schemes, both social and political. Like Warren Harding before him, Jimmy Carter, an obscure southern governor, won the White House by dodging the issues and promising to restore trust in government and faith in our system. Sort of a "return to normalcy," although not quite.

Carter's presidency was fraught with problems. Keynesian economics had come back to haunt the American people. Keynes's prescriptions had given the politicians license to institute huge spending programs. The promises the politicians had made became more and more burdensome and the result was the great inflation which threatened to bring down the curtain on economic growth. Something different was going on from what occurred in past Kondrateiff upswings. The steep recession of 1973-74, unlike the contraction of 1920-21, had not stopped inflation so that the plateau period of noninflationary growth could growth could commence. Although the fires of inflation had been banked, they flared up with even more intensity in the late 1970s. There was an inflationary interlude than, during this up wave, lasted for almost nine years.

By 1980 the dollar was in freefall, inflation was running at about 15 percent on a yearly basis and appeared out of control, the prime rate of interest was over 20 percent, gold was trading at over $800 an ounce, the price of oil was soaring and Iran, a third rate power, held 239 U.S. citizens hostage, while the world's mightiest nation stood by helplessly.

Enter Reganomics

Not to worry, Ronald Reagan would soon march triumphantly into the White House with a promise to restore the old maligned values and unchain business from the straight jacket that Keynesian economics had imposed upon it. He boldly put forward a program directed at freeing markets and increasing competition.

Reaganomics attempted to stimulate the economy via tax cuts, deregulation, and curbing government spending. It worked. Inflation flagged and the wheels of American industry began rolling once again. The Reagan boom of the 1980s bears a striking resemblance to the 1920s. For seven fat years the boom rolled on and produced real growth averaging 3½ percent a year. This was the second longest cyclical expansion in post-World War history. It spawned a new breed of small and nimble concerns. An estimated five million new businesses incorporated between 1982 and 1990. Trendy boutiques and eateries were crowded with yuppies who seemed to have bottomless pockets.

Chapter Four

Stock prices soared into the wild blue yonder. Real estate prices rose to absolutely incredible levels, while interest rates and the price of oil did a swan dive.

Yet, things were not as rosy as they appeared. This plateau period, like those in previous Kondratieff up waves, was built on a foundation of sand. Serious recession in 1973-1975 and again in 1981-1982 had not solved the problems that arose during the long expansion. The economy had been propped up before the deflation had run its natural course. This portion of the expansion had begun with the cost of capital and labor too high and the desire to be a risk taker much too strong. The economic climate had turned unfriendly to business, although most people didn't recognize it. The agriculture sector, raw materials, such as oil, and smokestack America were brought to their knees. The oil patch, from Texas to Colorado, was in depression throughout much of the 1980s. Across the Pacific Ocean, a mighty competitor was flexing its economic muscle and challenging American industries dominance. Japan was flooding the world's major markets with a tidal wave of autos, steel and electronic goods. The Savings and Loans industry collapsed and had to be bailed out by the taxpayers to the tune of nearly 300 billion dollars. Corporate raiders, green mailers, white knights, and arbitrageurs strode over our financial landscape dismantling and restructuring businesses and in the process raking in bushel baskets full of money.

In October 1987 stocks experienced a one-day fall of horrifying proportions. The socialist economies of the Soviet Union and Eastern Europe collapsed and with it their governments. By the end of the decade profits for most American business firms were in decline. In late 1991 corporate profits turned lower and continued to sag for five straight quarters—the longest such period since the 1930s. To many, the 1980s appeared to be a decade of greed, wherein the rich got richer and nearly everyone else was left behind.

The economy was able to stay afloat only because of an enormous buildup in debt, both government and private, which has, however, left the financial structure trembling. Hordes of American consumers invaded the nation's stores and shopping malls with the battle cry, "charge it." Reagan turned Keynesian economics on its head and ran up gargantun budget deficits. The national debt quaudrupled in the Reagan-Bush years to $4 trillion. Allowing the deficit to reach truly alarming figures ensured that the Democrats could no longer legislate huge government spending programs. Of course, it has also dismantled our arsenal of Keynesian counter cyclical tools.

Yet, these realities were ignored by many investors. Like their grandfathers a half century ago, they put on rose-colored glasses and went on a stock-buying spree on the assumption lower inflation and interest rates would bring back the glory days of the 1950s and 1960s.

Recession Hits—and Stays

In 1990 recession struck again. By most statistics it was quite mild. However, real estate values crumbled. Commercial real estate which had enjoyed a 40-odd year boom since World War II with nary a setback, fell an estimated 30 percent from its peak in the late '80s. Officially the recession ended in March 1991, but almost no one believed it. The economy has been unable to generate the head of steam it usually does when coming out of a recession. It has been the slowest recovery since the Great Depression and jobs keep disappearing not just for the duration, but for good. It took eight successive quarters of growth for output to reach the level it held before the recession began in the summer of 1990. This is more than twice as long as the average post-World War II recovery. Furthermore, unemployment seems stuck at about 7 percent or so, way above its pre-recession level. The Fed has done its bit and pushed interest rates to the floor. However, the economy has not been so unresponsive to Fed stimulation since the 1930s and as in that earlier period, a sense of danger hangs like smoke in the air. The optimism of the 1980s has given way to fear of the future. The thud we have all heard is the sound of Donald Trump, the Reichmann brothers, and scores of lessor successful people hitting the ground.

The chances are we have begun another down wave in the Kondratieff cycle. This obviously has dire implications to a people who have grown up in a period of constantly rising prices. Chances are we will come face to face with a falling price level and will learn that this latter environment is not so kind to businesses and investors. We will be surprised by the length and nastiness of the breaks in almost every market, including stocks and real estate, and legions of investors will in all probability be badly bloodied. The wheel of fortune has turned.

Sometime during the next decade the Dow Jones Industrial Average will fall to a level at least 50 percent below its all-time peak. Huge numbers of American corporations and American lives are likely to be reshaped. The weak sisters of the computer industry should be weeded out, and the importance of the automobile industry is likely to be drastically curtailed and there is likely to be a huge falloff in corporate earnings. Cyclical expansions during this time are likely to be either brief or tepid. We will not be able to pursue a new investment theme until our commitments of capital, labor, and resources to the main investment themes of the past up wave have been reduced. And this cutting back means destroying businesses, jobs, and capital which is sure to be a very painful process.

However don't look for a Great Depression. This is because this slump follows the second upswing of this 100-year cycle. As a result, the mechanisms put in place to cushion the economy from a repeat of the 1930s are likely to work and we will not witness the killer down wave that some of the Kondratieff people are looking for. The levels of bankruptcies, unemployment, and debt reduction will in all probability fall far short of those reached in the 1930s. Nor will the falloff in the price level be anywhere near as steep as that of 60 years ago. This period will probably resemble the hard times Britain experienced at the end of the last century. My best guess is that when we look back on it we will characterize it as a long period of economic stagnation, rather than a great collapse.

On the other hand, the speculative craze and overexpansion of industry in Japan got way out of hand in the 1980s and as such, they are vulnerable to a much deeper slump. Eastern Europe, whose economies have already collapsed, are experiencing special problems and it would be no surprise if the situation over there got quite ugly during this period.

Chapter Four

Social Mood Will Shift

We can expect a shift in the social mood which will change America's life styles, tastes and moral values. The avoidance of pain will become the dominant theme in people's behavior. They will adopt a mindset that emphasizes caution and is willing to settle for less. Their focus will be on security and cooperation. Safe, unadventurous jobs will be back in demand. We can expect a noticeable moderation in the cultural revolution. In all probability, women will lower their skirts, tighten their morals, and become more willing to assume the "traditional" female roles. And the younger generation will be less rebellious and less scornful of marriage and family life. Drug usage will probably diminish, along with sexual adventurousness.

The various social causes which sprang to life during the '60s and '70s are likely to be replaced by a coalescence behind an important new cause, that is, the elimination of the culprit responsible for the economic turbulence. Although we are not likely to begin another Puritan revolution, or for that matter, return to the social conventions of the 1950s, the United States at the beginning of the twenty-first century will most likely be a more socially conservative nation than it was in the 1980s.

The laws of nature have caught up with the American people. They are finding out that they are subject to the same laws of rise and decline as every other nation. Up to this point we have dealt with these Kondratieff waves as if they were very much alike. However such is not the case. Although they are similar, there are important differences depending upon if they are the first or second wave in a greater 100-year cycle.

THE GREAT CYCLE
● ● ● ● ● ●

Since the advent of the industrial revolution in the late eighteenth century there have been four Kondratieff cycles. However they do not look exactly alike. These cycles have some important differences. This is because two Kondratieff cycles form a great cycle which lasts for about a century.

A 100-year cycle begins with an important new addition to the resource base. Basic resources consist of foodstuffs, raw materials, and energy, and are an important part of the economy. It is only when these resources are both cheap and plentiful that we are able to begin a phase of rapid industrialization. When some nation makes an important new discovery that broadens and cheapens its resource base, it gains a comparative economic advantage which it will ride to world economic and political leadership. This resource advantage is soon transformed into an innovating industry, which by creating its own market, intensifies the process of industrialization, such as the automobile. After a generation or so of rising economic prosperity, a struggle for world dominance breaks out. This will be a long and bitter conflict and the nation in control of, the new resource usually emerges victorious and becomes the leader of a new world order. This display of military might impresses the contending powers so that they acquiesce to the new political pecking order. Consequently, the remainder of the 100-year period is likely to be relatively peaceful, at least for the dominant power. Further wars which involve that power are likely to be contained and on the whole not very bloody or destructive.

Following the successful conclusion of the war, the people of the new dominant nation recognize they are at the top of the heap and become wide-eyed optimists. They go on a rampage of speculation which throws a rosy glow of endless abundance over the economy and encourages an expansion in industrial capacity way out of proportion to potential demand.

This precipitates a depression of terrifying proportions. Factories lay idle, trade dries up, and legions of the working class are reduced to a wretched existence. This unexpected economic and social upheaval causes the nation to destroy its old order and restructure its economy and political system.

Following this major depression, a second Kondratieff upswing begins and ushers in a period of undreamed-of prosperity. An important change in the direction of industrialization takes place. For instance, in the 1960s a revolution in knowledge replaced a 100-year revolution in transportation as the energizing force of industrialization. This second upswing differs from the first in that this time, prosperity is more widespread. The prosperity spreads to other nations which begin to industrialize. And the leading country does not experience either a speculative bubble or a vast over-expansion of industry. People come to believe that the new structure imposed upon the economy during the depression is responsible for the prosperity. Although there is usually a war during the up phase of this cycle, it is not likely to be a major one. This is because no one is likely to mount a serious challenge to the leading power which is at the height of its glory. The glow of a golden prosperity along with the long-held perceptions of her military might make her look invincible.

After about a generation of increasing and spreading prosperity, extreme competitive pressures develop and a fierce struggle for markets begin. A growing demand for foodstuffs, raw materials, and energy outstrips the resource base, puting an end to the period of cheap and abundant resources. About the same time, the structure imposed upon the economy during the prior depression begins generating insurmountable problems. These problems put the economy in a bind and precipitate a second slump, which is milder than the previous one. The mechanisms which were put into effect after the crushing depression 50 years earlier cushion the blow. The memory of that spectacular collapse spurs the major players to make accommodations to hold the economy together.

A Look at 100-Year Cycles

This pattern extends back to the late 16th century and perhaps earlier. Let us sketch the history of the past 400 years with this century long cycle in mind. The first 100-year cycle begins in France in the 1590s. King Henry IV, spends huge sums of money to reclaim marshes and build canals, roads, and bridges. The French communications system becomes the best in Europe and induces a vast agricultural prosperity. The surplus of cheap food allows France to develop industries, such as cloth, glass making, and iron. A pronounced upswing in commercial and industrial activity follows. Cities become larger. Prices, which have been rising since the great discoveries of gold and silver 100 years earlier, go through the roof. Soon Henry's desire for "every family (to) have a fowl in the pot on Sunday," seems within reach. It is a time of giddy expenditures, splendid building, gigantic feasts, and lavish evanescent shows. France's economic strength soon surpasses that of Spain, who was the dominant power at the end of the 17th century and they face off against one another in the 30 Year War, which most historians consider to be the bloodiest and most savage in history.

In the 1620s a bone chilling depression begins and puts an end to a century long period of rising prices. Production of cloth just about comes to a halt, and many of the leading enterprises of that day, including soap boiling, ship building, glass making, and iron shut down for lack of markets.

68

This period of economic distress lasts for about 20 years and there is widespread social discontent and suffering among all classes of society. Contemporaries write of the deplorable conditions of French industry at the ascension of Louis XIV in 1643.

France emerges from the 30 Year War as the leading European power and begins to transform her political and economic structure. Louis imposes absolute monarchy on the people. The composition of the economy is altered. Colbert, Minister of Finance, goes way beyond the early mercantilist ideas that one country's gain is another's loss. He introduces a comprehensive code of regulation to direct production and trade in the interests of the state and close off markets to competitors.

This strict form of mercantilism is the first experiment of a modern controlled economy, and is soon followed by economic revival and a long period of commercial growth and wealth creation. French products acquire a reputation for the highest quality and the most fashionable style during the second half of the 17th century. To be sure, much of the new wealth goes into unproductive investment and luxury consumption. Nevertheless, French landlords and merchants think the formula for economic success has been found, and gain confidence in the future. The French economy becomes the model for other nations to copy. The English economy in particular, shows real life and becomes France's chief commercial rival.

However, in the 1680s the economies of Europe press up against the limits of their resource base. The great forests in many parts of Western Europe are shrinking, and a shortage of timber precipitates the first modern energy crisis. The price of wood rises to exorbitant levels, constricting further economic expansion in France. A second slump begins. The value of land falls; the number of beggars rises; and tax collections fall far below the amounts reached in Colbert's day.

During the following 15 years, the air is filled with an atmosphere of gloom. However, commercial and industrial activity do not skid to a complete halt as they did in the 1630s. Nor are the peasants reduced to the level of suffering and misery experienced 50 years earlier.

At this point in the cycle, the leading economic nations search for solutions. Because of the restricting structure that Colbert had imposed on the economy, France experiences a loss of creative energy and is not in a position to develop the new resources. Strict mercantilism has come back to haunt the French people. England, however, where almost all the great forests had been cut down, responds to the timber crises by developing her vast coal supplies and intensifying her search for overseas trade and resources.

Rise of Bourgeoisie, Puritanism

England is in a position to develop the resources because a civil war in the late seventeenth century has freed a new social class, the bourgeoisie, who are more motivated and willing to take the economic risks necessary to exploit the new sources of economic growth. A political realignment with the freeing of a new social class seems to be a necessary precondition to achieve economic mastery. The English Civil War, which is a revolt against the free spending and loose living ways of the upper class, produces the social and economic mobility, that enables Britain to develop her vast coal supplies which will replace timber as the chief source of energy. This internal upheaval also ushers in the ideas of Puritanism. The values of thrift, temperance sobriety, industry, duty, self discipline, and delayed gratification will gain ascendancy during the next two centuries and provide the underpinnings to a bourgeois social and economic system. By the end of the 19th century people of the industrial economies will thoroughly believe that there is an important connection between these values and worldly success.

In the late 1690s a second 100-year cycle begins, spurred on by the exploitation of cheap coal in England, which joins with Scotland in 1707 to become Great Britain. At the beginning of the 18th century the British economy shows new energy. Signs of growing wealth, trade, and industry are visible everywhere one looks. Shopkeepers are appearing in nearly every village. Shortly after France refuses to give England commercial trading privileges in Spanish America, tensions mount and erupt in the War of Spanish Succession. This is the bloodiest conflict since the 30 Year War. In one battle alone there are 20,000 casualties, which to the English people seems to be "butchery." Britain is the apparent victor, but the war concludes before France is brought to her knees. Britain becomes the leading economic nation but this time the question of world political leadership is not settled and throughout the rest of the century France continues to make bids for political dominance and remains England's chief commercial rival. This period is to be the least stable or peaceful in this 400-year period.

Following the War of Spanish Succession there is a period of intense speculation in Britain, which culminates in the infamous South Sea Bubble. Shares of the South Sea Company, which had originally been priced at 100 pounds, rise to a breathtaking 1,050 pounds. Stories are bandied about of beggars becoming rich overnight. Dozens of new companies of a speculative nature—including such schemes as wheels of perpetual motion, making salt water fresh, turning sea water into gold, and finally, for "an undertaking of great advantage, but nobody to know what it is"—are organized and sell stock. Almost everyone from dukes and princes to men of the street take part. Then in 1720 the crash hits. With a sickening thud shares of the South Sea Company fall to 120 pounds, and most of the other companies become worthless. Over 30 members of Parliament, including many of its leaders, are found to have been bribed. Thousands of people are ruined and London rocks with scandal and dismay. This financial crisis is followed by severe agricultural depression, and a long period of retardation in trade and commerce. A malaise hangs over most British industries throughout much of the second quarter of the 18th century

An important transformation of Britain's government and economy takes place. Cabinet government is implemented and this curbs the authority of the King and begins the slow evolution toward democracy. Britain also takes a giant economic step and breaks away from a 200-year tradition of increasing state control over commercial activity. She dismantles some of the prohibitions and regulations which are hampering trade in the domestic markets and begins to practice a more relaxed form of mercantilism. This unleashes a wave of creativity and inventiveness and gives new life to British commerce and industry.

Development of Cheaper Materials

In England during the mid–1740s there is a striking growth in the output of iron, due to substitution of coke for charcoal in the smelting process. It is the first real modern technological breakthrough and begins a 100-year revolution in the development of cheaper materials, which will progress from iron to cotton. A new breed of iron masters make fortunes and arouse the hope of gain. There is a new zeal for commerce and trade. Merchants accustomed to the routine of mercantilism and state protection are pushed aside. France's economy also gets a lift. However it has not had the social upheaval necessary to allow a middle class to prosper and grow. An ancient regime, a class of unproductive aristocrats and bureaucrats, remains in control and their extravagance sucks the wealth out of the whole country.

The vitality of the British economy surprises most everyone. A body of intellectuals take notice and attribute the astonishing economic success to the retreat from strict mercantilism. One of these thinkers, Adam Smith, publishes a treatise, "The Wealth of Nations," which claims that if a nation completely dismantles its regulation and control of the economy, the result will be an undreamed of prosperity. Pretty strong stuff for that day.

This dazzling economic performance comes to an end in the late 1760s as problems very similar to those which occurred at the end of the seventeenth century appear. Once again the growth of a pre-industrial economy is checked by an insufficient resource base. In this case most of the water power sites, which are limited by the number of streams available, are already taken up. This, of course, puts a damper on further growth. A period of economic stagnation and hard times follows. This period of adversity, though painful, is not nearly so debilitating as in the 1730s. This is partly due to the fact that Britain is already beginning to develop steam power, which is about to emancipate industry from its dependence on unreliable water power, and transform Britain into the first modern industrial society. The development of steam power allows Britain to transform her vast coal supplies into a new source of energy and remain on top for another century. France also experiences hard times during the 1760s and 1770s. However her response is quite different. Following an internal upheaval, the French revolution, Napoleon, mounted on a white horse, leads his armies across Europe in a new bid for world mastery.

Industrial Revolution Launched

Sometime in the mid 1780s Britain begins another 100-year cycle. With the application of steam power to the cotton loom, the industrial revolution is launched. Britain puts an end to Napoleon's trouble-making early on and achieves world political leadership. After shipping him off to St. Helena, England finds it in her best interests to pursue commerce peacefully and for the rest of that century engages in only minor foreign involvements which do not get out of hand. Following the war there is a flurry of speculative activity and over-expansion of the cotton mills. This results in a terrible period of depression, a period that could be called England's "creative destruction," a term coined by the economist, Joesph Schumpeter.

We call it a creative destruction because the excess debt and productive capacity acquired during the prior up wave were eliminated so that the second great application of steam power, the railroad, is able to attract the capital and labor necessary to germinate and bloom. The misery of the 1830s and 40s brings on a mandate to overhaul the British political-economic system so as to prevent another major slump. Legislation is passed to free the economy from the archaic restrictions and controls presumed responsible for the depression, and Britain achieves commercial freedom. The Liberal party becomes the dominant political force and remains so throughout the remainder of the century.

In 1848, a 25-year golden age of prosperity begins. The age of cotton passes, and the age of the railroad commences. Other nations, particularly Germany and the U.S., follow Britain's lead and experience an economic takeoff. Darwin publishes his "Origin Of The Species," which provides the rationale to a new secular materialistic world outlook, which in turn launches a social revolution of vast importance. During the following upswings of the cycle the old Puritan values of temperance, sobriety, frugality, industry, and personal responsibility slowly lose their force. They are replaced with values which emphasize pleasure, hedonism, instant gratification, and entitlement, and as such are more in tune with the new view of the world.

Chapter Five

The U.S. undergoes a bitter Civil War which sends prices skyrocketing. The inflationary impact of the war provides the stimulus to quicken industrial activity in Britain and heighten expectations. These expectations are cooled. The overbuilding of the railroads begins and soon the investment opportunities based on the further application of steam power are exhausted. By 1873 Britain's economy has outstripped its resource base and is ready to crumble; however, this time the situation is quite different from the bust of a half-century earlier or, for that matter, from the crash of 1929.

The industrial leaders are now a leadership class and are committed to the ongoing prosperity. They resolve not to let a period of bloodletting, like that experienced after the Napoleonic wars, occur. They are unwilling to scrap everything and begin anew, so, rather than permit a creative destruction, they promote a massive effort to patch up the system before the excesses are fully liquidated. Money from the big banks is channeled to the railroads, coal companies, and iron works, thus preventing the widespread bankruptcies and debt reduction which usually occurs during a creative destruction. The beast of depression is tamed somewhat, without the spectacular collapse that occurred during the prior depressionary period. The captains of industry feel more secure, since they are able to maintain control of the capital assets. However, they are no longer willing to take the economic risks necessary to develop innovations. Because the class structure has solidified, it becomes harder for a new class of innovators and entrepreneurs to acquire the money and financing to develop the new ideas. As a consequence, the creative genius of the nation is lost, and innovations are increasingly tried elsewhere.

U.S. Becomes World Leader

Germany and the United States have already adopted England's methods and techniques, such as the development of the railroad, and are in a better position to exploit these innovations. Both Germany and America have benefited from an earlier political upheaval in the 19th century, which has produced a realignment of political power. The United States, however, is also the beneficiary of cheap and abundant agriculture and an influx of immigrants, provided by the huge migrations to the United States in the latter part of the 19th century. Consequently she is in a better position than Germany to become the new leader. She is able to adopt a new source of energy, electric power, which enables her to exploit the worlds vast supplies of oil. This provides her with a comparative advantage.

A fourth 100-year cycle begins in about 1897. It will be the United States' century. The electric power she has developed will soon be used to ignite the internal combustion engine and support a wide range of further innovation. Germany, on the other hand, is tied to the new chemical industry that is not related to a new source of energy. As this cycle begins Great Britain, still the world leader, feels the pressure of both the younger German and United States economies closing in on her. Tensions mount and Germany calls Britain's bluff as the world leader. Once again, there is sparring for world hegemony. The result is World War I, and as Britain is unable to beat back the German challenge, the United States comes to her aid. As world leadership hangs in the balance, this war, unlike smaller wars, has to be won decisively. Although ravaged, Germany does not acquiesce to the United States' claim to dominance. When she is able, Germany breaks the Armistice and wages war again, just as Napoleon had returned to wage his 100-day campaign. The United States has to put an end to this persistent pretender. During these periods of war, Britain rather silently exits from center stage; the British phase of the industrial revolution ends, and the United States inherits the mantle of world leadership.

The United States emerges from World War I with heightened expectations, cools these expectations, and then goes on a wild speculative binge and proceeds to overbuild the automobile industry. There is a great deal of industrial over expansion. The period of creative destruction is upon the United States.

Like England a hundred years earlier, the United States lacks experience in such matters and is not prepared for deep depression. Consequently, the excesses are rather fully liquidated. There is a relative redistribution of capital assets. That is, a lot of people lose their money, and other people with good economic ideas can acquire assets.

The structure of the economy is altered ending a 200-year trend of increasing commercial freedom. The government adopts the ideas of John Maynard Keynes. Keynes was concerned about long periods of insufficient demand or diminished purchasing power, which every so often brought a laissez-faire economy to a grinding halt. His contention was that by giving the government the responsibility to create the purchasing power necessary to regenerate confidence, we could, and in the interest of humaneness we should, put our resources back to work sooner than the natural forces in the economy would dictate. This would isolate the economy from future depressions. Essentially, this was Keynes's message. The Democratic party catches on and very quickly incorporates it into its political program and becomes the dominate political party for the next 50 years.

Age of Computer Replaces Age of Auto

Soon the United States begins a second Kondratieff cycle. It begins with a period of golden prosperity wherein the industrial promises of the past 50 years are largely fulfilled. The age of the auto is replaced by the age of the computer. The inflationary impact of the Vietnam war helps to heighten expectations in the United States. And these heightened expectations have to be cooled.

The ongoing social revolution is carried further, perhaps to the point of moral anarchy. The long-held idea of personal responsibility comes under blistering attack from the descendants of both Keynes and Freud. On the one hand psychologists tell us we are not responsible for our actions and on the other hand economists propose giving economic responsibility to the government. The result is the growing belief in entitlement. That is, we are entitled to a job, health care, social security, a college education, welfare payments, and on and on.

Other countries follow in America's economic footsteps. In particular, Japan and Germany become important business rivals to the U.S. and put intense competitive pressures on her. Keynesian economics begins to cause unintended problems. The price of oil and other resources skyrockets, sending out the message that once again we have outrun our resource base. The world economy including the U.S.

begins to grow at a slower clip and this is where we are now (see Figure 5–1).

Each great cycle is composed of two Kondratieff waves. These waves are somewhat different. In the first wave the expansionary phase ends with a speculative bubble and a vast over-expansion of industry. This is followed by a spectacular collapse of the economy, which throws a cloud of gloom across the nation. The response is a restructuring of the economy.

The second Kondratieff wave ushers in a golden age of prosperity. The expansionary phase of this wave does not produce a speculative bubble or over-expansion in capacity in the leading country to anywhere near the extent that, it occurred during the first wave. The problems this time result largely because the huge buildup in worldwide output has outstripped the world economy's resource base. The economic slump which follows does not turn into a great collapse like in the one following the first wave. The prior restructuring provides immunity and the nation is able to patch things up before they get out of hand. Consequently, the structure of the economy is not changed in a significant way.

This great cycle results from the collective reactions of people to a new technological development, and produces a pattern of growth, crisis, renewal—a so-called golden age—and finally decline. But keep in mind that these are not just repetitive cycles. Rather they are progressive in that each one ascends to a higher level.

Let us try to answer the question of why there are Kondratieff cycles.

Figure 5-1

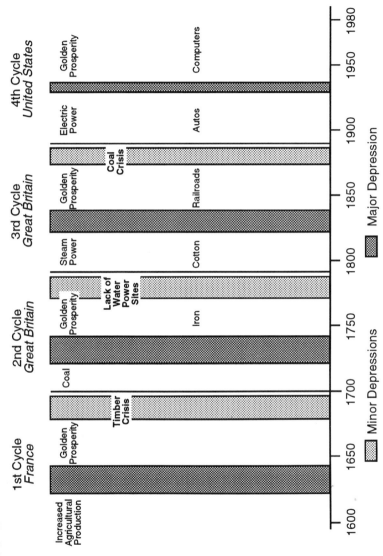

MASS PSYCHOLOGY: THE KEY TO CYCLES

• • • • • • •

Human behavior is different from what we have been taught. Human beings are not objective creatures as we like to think. We are not economic individuals who act in our own rational self-interest. Rather, we are *psychological beings*, conditioned by our experiences, especially those experiences which serve as important lessons of pain or pleasure. When some lesson of pain—say, an economic depression—deflates our self-image, we perceive the world as risky. On the flip side, when some lesson of pleasure— such as a long period of prosperity—inflates our self-image, the world no longer appears so risky. These resulting perceptions of risk are the shared assumptions through which we see the world. These *assumptions color the way we think and act.* In one case, we attempt to avoid pain, while in another we seek to pursue pleasure, and in so doing, become receptive to ideas, beliefs, and attitudes which rationalize these actions.

Following an extended period of prosperity, men and women adopt the psychology of affluence and its byproduct, economic optimism, wherein they enjoy life, have fun, and become economic risk takers. This mass psychology of optimism, once set off, takes on a life of its own and continues until people become excessively optimistic. This psychology influences economic events in its direction, and this in turn induces other people to adopt corresponding beliefs and expectations. They rationalize that what has happened will continue to happen, and thus come to see less risk than actually exists. Consequently, too many people become risk takers, which in turn creates the conditions for a big bust. This bust, or depression, then sets off a psychology of pessimism which continues until people see more risk than really exists. At that point too many people become risk averters, and this lays the foundation for a long period of economic expansion. In each case, the process usually occurs in three stages.

The last expansionary phase began in 1949, during a time when people were excessively pessimistic (see Figure 2–1). The long period of economic pain that followed the 1929 collapse had humbled people. They came to see the world as a risky place and became skeptical of the economy's ability to provide prosperity. People cut their economic commitments to the bone and delayed consumption in order to build up savings. In short, most people became risk averters.

However, as the expansion of the 1950s rolled on, with nothing more than minor setbacks to interrupt it, a number of people recognized the emerging prosperity and began changing their behavior to coincide with it. They dipped into their savings in order to buy stocks and real estate, to become entrepreneurs, and to increase consumption. They became risk takers. As the success of these new risk takers was recognized, others joined in. They increased their spending for both business and consumption purposes. The expansion was being fed.

Yet, the vast majority of people hung on to a perception of a risky world acquired during the depression, and remained risk averters. By the late 1950s, the rise in the price of assets and cost of doing business left the economy unable to recruit new risk takers and no longer able to generate the spending increases necessary to support the aggressive building of inventories and capital items that had taken place. The expansion had gotten ahead of itself and was vulnerable to a setback. This ended the first stage of the *expansionary phase.*

Refueling the Expansion

As business profits fell and the stock market began slipping, some of the overextended risk takers were forced to liquidate. In 1960-1961 there was a contraction followed in 1962 by a sharp break in the stock market. This was the most serious run of events than had occurred since the late 1940's. Fears of 1929 were revived.

Chapter Six

Yet, in 1962, things were different. The protracted and unexpected period of prosperity provided a lesson of pleasure, which undermined the shared assumptions of a risky world. Many risk averters had been impressed by this run of prosperity, but were only willing to commit themselves to it provided they could do so on favorable terms,i.e., when the price of assets and the costs of doing business had a big fall-off. The contraction of 1960-1961 provided such an opportunity. The willingness of these people to dip into their savings and increase their economic commitments helped cushion this contraction and fueled another expansion.

As the economy and stock market began to recover in 1962 without having fallen into depression, more risk averters became convinced that the prosperity was for real and began to join in. The increased spending by an influx of new risk takers broadened the expansion and sent the stock market soaring to all-time highs. Suddenly, people from all walks of life began to notice that the economy was continuing to exceed their expectations. In an attempt to explain this phenomenon, the media and academe put the economy under their huge microscopes. They discovered that because of the government's commitment to maintain the level of demand, we could now expect continual prosperity. They spread the message: we had entered a new economic age, one that was quite different from that of the '30s.

The majority of people became optimistic that prosperity would last, and this changed *the psychological environment*. The world no longer appeared to be so risky and, as a result, people became less concerned with avoiding pain and more interested in pursuing pleasure and participating in the good life. In order to justify, or rationalize, this change in their behavior, they readjusted their beliefs. They adopted the belief that they were entitled to enjoy life and grew impatient with the old societal constraints which they felt had in the past kept them from achieving personal fulfillment. In short, a vast psychological change had occurred which led to a world that moved to a different beat—very much faster, louder, and more optimistic than in the 1930s.

In the economic sphere, the majority of people became risk takers. Some became entrepreneurs; others acquired stocks and real estate, and still others cut into their savings so that they could increase their standard of living. Of course, these actions furthered the expansion even more, again pleasantly surprising people.

Economic Models Break Down in '60s

Yet, this new psychological environment soon had an important but unseen effect on the economy. One economist after the other, from Walter Heller to Milton Friedman, complained that their economic models which, of course, were based on the long psychological environment of 1938-1965, were no longer working. In 1968, Dr. Arthur Burns, who was chairman of the National Bureau of Economic Research, summed up the situation when he sadly commented, "The rules of economics are not working the same way they used to, the substantial sharp raises in wages . . . contrasts markedly with our experience in earlier recessions."

What had happened was that there had been a change in the way people were acting. This change began to undermine the very foundation upon which our long prosperity rested. Owing largely to an abundant amount of cheap or relatively cheap capital, labor, raw materials, fuel, and food, along with a relative shortage of industrial capacity, all of which had been the legacy of the prior depression, business profits for a long time had been rather easy to come by. This, in turn, had helped encourage the capital formation process. Now, however, with the advent of the new risk takers and the increased demand they generated, the cost of capital, labor, and raw materials skyrocketed; the long-term rate of interest surpassed the natural rate of interest. Because of these escalating costs and an increase in industrial capacity, this climate in which business profits were easy to attain ended. The capital formation process was impaired, and, by the early 1970s, pockets of weakness, such as Lockheed, and New York City, began appearing in the economy. The performance of the economy had become poorer, and again we were vulnerable to a serious economic contraction and stock market break. Thus, the second stage of the expansionary phase ended.

As business activity slowed and the stock market sagged, some of the overextended risk takers, who now were more numerous than in 1961-1962, were forced to liquidate. We got another serious contraction, that of 1973-1974, along with a chilling break in the stock market. Once again fears were aroused that we were headed for a depression.

Although the economy was not as healthy as it had been in the 1950s, there were still many strong areas. They could bolster the weak joints so that the economy would remain on course. Money was channeled, through the banking system, from the many profitable areas of the economy to New York City, Lockheed and many of the less-developed countries (to help offset their increased costs of energy) so that these weaker companies, cities, and nations would not go under and drag the world economy down with them. The government also cut taxes so that aggregate demand would be increased. As a result, corporate profitability was restored at least temporarily, and we emerged from this serious contraction to begin another run of expansion.

However, the inability to slow the rapid advance in prices produced sub par economic growth in the late 1970s and we could not begin the plateau period. The period from 1974 to 1982 was an inflationary interlude. Another steep recession in 1981-82 finally cooled inflation and the plateau period began. During this third stage of the expansionary phase, the hard core risk averters joined in. They had missed out during the first and second stages and were aware that their views were out of step with the majority. These risk averters recognized that they were being left behind in the pursuit of the good life and as such were becoming uncomfortable with their convictions. Once the economy began another sustained economic advance, many of these people could no longer resist conforming to the lesson of pleasure. They became believers in the prosperity and started dipping into their savings to make investments and expand the level of their spending. This spending helped fuel the third and final stage of the up wave.

Too Many Risk Takers

By 1990 we had experienced three stages in the expansionary phase and most people had come to believe in the prosperity. The psychological environment had become overdone; that is, too many people now wanted to become risk takers. The excessive pessimism which characterized the 1940s had been replaced with an excessive optimism.

The economy was now ready for a huge bust. What had happened during the third stage was that as more and more people had come to believe, and rationalized this belief by arguing that "another depression could not possibly occur," the economy began to appear risk-free. The memory of a real depression was dimmed and there was a lack of appreciation of the real risk that did exist. Expectations became way too high in relation to what the economy could deliver.

Such an atmosphere results in a less cautious attitude among business people. The less qualified ones become entrepreneurs. The more promising investment ideas become exhausted and the less promising investment opportunities are pursued. Workers become less concerned about their jobs. We enter an atmosphere where business miscalculations increase, where overborrowing and overspending become prevalent, and where many people are willing to pay ever-increasing prices to acquire stocks, real estate, or raw materials—that is, until they are no longer able to. The government can not prevent a collapse by cutting taxes or priming the pump because any new stimulus only enforces this same economic behavior; people increase their borrowing, bankers make more unsound loans, producers attempt to raise their prices even more, and so on—until something gives. Perhaps the price of energy rises too high, or maybe the number of unsound loans becomes enormous. Whatever it is, some problem finally becomes unmanageable and sets off a liquidation which shatters an overdone psychology.

Yet, one would think that this imbalance in the economy should be perceived. However, people believe in this prosperity and people who believe usually do not listen to arguments contrary to their belief, no matter how logical. Throughout the 1970s and 1980s, many doomsayers had cried "wolf" and the "wolf" had never come. Certainly we thought at the time that the high price of energy would choke off growth. We heard persuasive arguments that the huge budget deficits of the 1980s would soon bring the economy to its knees. Following the October 1987 collapse in the stock market, popular opinion had it that a bitter recession was on its way. These problems had been around for quite a while yet the economy had *not* turned down into a depression. People's experience had been one of continual economic expansion. Gradually, people came to see that the worst does not usually happen and do not buy the scare talk. When confronted by the doomsayers, the mass of people resort to faith, not logic, for, in this respect, faith seems the better guide. And, to change a belief which rests largely on faith, people must experience the opposite.

There is no way out short of a collapse. Behavior must be altered so that the excessive economic commitments are reduced, costs are lowered, liquidity is rebuilt, and expectations are shrunk. Such a change requires a lesson of pain—that is, a period of hard times.

The depressionary phase of the cycle also usually occurrs in three stages. That is what happened during the last depressionary period which began in 1929. In the first stage, the depression of 1929-1933 shattered an overdone psychological environment, one in which people had been excessively optimistic. During the subsequent recovery in the economy, a lot of people who had been affected by the wrenching lesson of pain eased out of their economic commitments, or at least refrained from increasing their spending. As a result, we got another economic contraction of major proportions in 1937, which was the beginning of the second stage down. During this stage, the majority of people became disillusioned and lost faith in the economy. The psychological environment changed to one where people now wanted to be risk averters.

This new psychology of pessimism affected people's willingness to spend and invest and as a result we got yet another fairly serious contraction, that of 1945-1946. It was the third stage down, and during it people became excessively pessimistic. Too many people had become risk averters and took precautions against another severe contraction and this built into the economy an immunity to further depression. Business costs fell dramatically, productive capacity was reduced, a hoard of liquidity was built up and a backlog of promising investment opportunities accumulated. This soon led to a real improvement in the performance of the economy.

Depression and Stagnation Provide Necessary Lessons

These periods of economic stagnation or depression play an important part in our world. They are not a malfunction of a capitalistic economy but, rather, a necessary lesson of pain which, by changing behavior, allows the economy to regenerate itself. What happens is that during good times, our beliefs and expectations become overdone. That is, too many people attempt to take advantage of economic growth. People, or at least some people, must be jolted back to reality once again. It takes an alternate lesson to do this, a lesson of pain if people have been dancing to the tune of pleasure. On the other hand if the people are responding to pain it takes a lesson of pleasure to change behavior. Most economists do not understand that we cannot alter behavior without causing some accompanying lesson of pain or pleasure.

Perhaps a certain amount of human suffering may be the price that must be paid for social and economic progress. If new ways of doing things are to emerge, power, at least over capital assets, must be passed from one group to another. Unfortunately, this is not likely to happen without chaos or conflict. Had our ancestors been able to avoid conflict and maintain a state of social harmony, the economic colossus upon which our contemporary civilization is based would not exist and in effect we would not be "we."

Because human psychology is slow to change, a broad economic move usually occurs in three stages. The first stage begins when some unexpected event shatters an overdone psychological environment. Yet, while some people respond immediately to this new lesson, most people find it outside their past experience and resist it. They need more evidence, that is, a second stage, wherein the experience is repeated. Typically, the majority become convinced during the second stage and this changes the psychological background. People begin to act differently, and this behavior soon affects the performance of the economy.

However, people are not likely to recognize this underlying change in the economy. Having just adopted a particular belief in the economy, they will be slow to change their minds. For example, most people do not begin abandoning their economic commitments during a contraction following the second stage of an expansionary phase. As a result, we get a third stage up, during which the diehards join in. The psychological environment becomes overdone, and the resulting economic behavior provides a fertile breeding ground for some contrary economic event, which, by shattering this overdone psychology, begins an important and extended economic move. Many, perhaps most, of the important moves in the economy, the stock market, and commodities are preceded by excessive optimism or excessive pessimism.

What happens is that people do catch on to the meaning of the important events and bring their beliefs and expectations into line with such experiences. However, as the majority of people finally recognize what is happening and adopt corresponding beliefs and expectations, these beliefs and expectations become overdone. This catching-on process, thus, results in a paradox: When too many people catch on to some economic event they change their behavior and this in turn, creates the conditions to undermine the event. This is a law of nature.

Some Lessons Learned Too Well

People, or at least the majority of people, are victims of their experience. They see things in light of what has happened in the past and commit themselves to one phase of a cycle. Like most politicians and generals, they find themselves continually fighting the last war. So, perhaps we learn the lessons, or at least some of the lessons, of history too well.

There is a tug of war between the conservative and adventurous members of society and each of us is assigned a role to play. At times it pays to be adventurous and lead the pack into some new and important area, while at other times it pays to be conservative. However, being the last to adopt either a adventurous or conservative posture usually does not pay. The continuing struggle between these two elements has helped prevent us from adopting or incorporating some new some new idea or way of doing things prematurly, and as such has kept our social evolution steady and smooth.

Let us now turn our attention to the shape of a Kondratieff wave.

Chapter Seven
• • • • • •

THE POLITICAL FACTOR AND THE ECONOMY
• • • • • • •

There are two leading political parties in the U. S. and each takes a different approach in dealing with the economy. In 1896 William Jennings Bryan, the Democratic party nominee for president summed up the difference between the parties. "There are two ideas of government. There are those who believe that, if you will only legislate to make the well-to-do prosperous, their prosperity will leak through to those below. The trickle down theory. The Democratic idea, however, has been that if you legislate to make the masses prosperous, their prosperity will find its way up through every class which rests upon them."

The Democratic party is the custodian of the American myth, the so-called "Democratic Ideal." This ideal, as stated by our forefathers in the Declaration of Independence, has it "that all men are created equal, that they are endowed by their creator with certain unalienable rights, that among these are the right to life, liberty and the pursuit of happiness." Myths are the binding glue of all civilizations and states. They provide a people with a shared view of the world. The Chinese had a myth, which was the mandate of heaven; the old Soviet Union had Marxism; Rome had the Republic, and the myth that pulls the American people together is the "Democratic Ideal."

The Democrats, as they see it, have a mission to improve the social and political life of the masses. To do so they push programs to protect and empower all groups, such as women, blacks, gays, the old, the poor, and the underprivileged.

In the realm of economics, the party of Franklin Delano Roosevelt embraced the Keynesian economic prescriptions early on, no doubt because they were compatible with their agenda of empowering the disadvantaged. The Democrats believe that the economy benefits most by increasing the purchasing power of the "little guys," the working class, farmers, and older people. The idea is that these people will increase their spending and this will bolster business profits, which in turn will induce business managers to increase their spending for capital items. This will keep the economy on a fast growth track.

Given this philosophy, Democratic administrations generally favor programs to create and maintain jobs and to provide subsidies to the needy, such as Social Security, food stamps, and price supports for farmers, while letting business and the well-to-do carry the burden of the tax load. They are also prone to hold business hostage to their social and regularity agenda, such as cleaning up the environment, providing child care or facilities for the handicapped. Of course, these policies lead to a rise in government spending and increasing budget deficits which, in turn, eventually have a profound inflationary impact on the economy.

Republican View Respects Marketplace

The Republicans, on the other hand, are skeptical of any scheme of affairs based on the perfectibility of man. They place a high priority on defending the social and moral order. They have a great deal of regard for our institutions and would not be quick to scuttle them. Republicans believe these structures have endured over a long period of time because there is a purpose inherent in them. The fact that we cannot perfectly explain why they work is not a defect in them but merely a limitation on us.

Members of the party of Abraham Lincoln, have an abiding respect for the market place. They consider it the most important American institution and gear their policies to protecting the integrity of that institution. Their goal is to provide a favorable investment climate, which includes a moderate tax load, stable prices, fewer government restrictions on business and the proper economic incentives so that business people will be encouraged to increase their investment. They believe that if businesses increase their spending the output of goods will multiply, more workers will be hired, wages will be boosted, and everyone will benefit. Stated another way, "a rising tide lifts all boats." As a result of this philosophy Republican administrations usually concentrate on lowering taxes, cutting government spending, reducing the regulatory burden on business, and preventing inflation—no matter the cost.

Which of these approaches works? Well, they both do—for a while, that is. During the 1950s, the Eisenhower administration cut taxes, reduced government spending and put the scourge of inflation to rest. Business executives responded by increasing their capital spending, which, in turn, created more jobs and propelled substantial advances in living standards. On the flip side of the coin, the Democrats, when they took over the reins of government in 1961, fostered programs to pump more spending money into the hands of the consumer. As a result, total purchasing power increased, providing the ammunition for the consumer buying spree that fueled the vigorous expansion of the 1960s.

What happens is that both approaches work because of the legacy inherited from the other party. Democratic administrations, leave a legacy of expanded consumer purchasing power. When the Republicans come in and generate a capital spending boom, the consumer has the wherewithal to keep up with the brisk growth in output. The result is a vigorous expansion, such as we had during the 1950s.

Republican Administrations, on the other hand, provide a legacy of low inflation, lessened government spending and a goodly amount of unused resources. This provides the subsequent Democratic administration plenty of room to expand the level of consumer purchasing power and government spending without igniting inflation. Once the new Administration puts money into the hands of the consumer the economy can pick up a head of steam, much as we saw throughout much of the 1960s.

Parties Take Policies Too Far

Yet, there is a problem in that each party pushes its approach too far; concentrating too much on one sector, either big business or the little guy, and neglecting the other. The initial success of a party's program usually provides a prospering economy, which leads to an easy reelection and what appears to be as a mandate for its policies. Since 1896, there have been nine times that the reins of government passed from one political party to the other. In eight of those times the party that had attained power won the following election, usually by an increased margin (see Table 7–1). Obviously, this was a vote of confidence for their new policies. However, with the re-election of the incumbent President, some of the more zealous members of the party are carried into office and the party's policies are pushed further.

Democratic administrations usually push their preoccupation with government spending and creating jobs too far. In addition, they have a strong tendency to look the other way when inflation begins upticking. Yet, after a while the Treasury's heavy borrowing makes it difficult to finance the investments needed to expand production, and supplies cannot keep pace with the boosts in consumption. Each period of Democratic reign has ended with a towering rise in the rate of inflation and a relative fall off in the rate of capital formation. It is then necessary to bring back

Table 7–1 Change in Political Parties

Date	Administration	Political Party	Percent of Popular Vote	Following Election	Percent of Popular Vote	Following Serious Contraction
1. 1896	McKinley/ T.Roosevelt	Rep	51.1%	1900	51.7%	1907
2. 1912	Wilson/ Marshall	Dem	41.9%	1916	49.3%	1920
3. 1920	Harding/ Coolidge	Rep	60.4%	1924	54.0%*	1929
4. 1932	F.D.Roosevelt/ Garner	Dem	57.4%	1936	60.8%	1937
5. 1952	Eisenhower/ Nixon	Rep	55.1%	1956	57.4%	1960
6. 1960	Kennedy/ Johnson	Dem	49.7%	1964	61.1%**	—
7. 1968	Nixon/ Agnew	Rep	43.4%	1972	60.7%	1973
8. 1976	Carter/ Mondale	Dem	50.4%	1980	41.9%***	—
9. 1980	Reagan/Bush	Rep	51.8%	1984	58.8%	1990
10. 1992	Clinton/ Gore	Dem	43.5%			

* Coolidge wins with 65% of the two party vote. La Follette, the progressive party candidate, captured 16.6% of popular vote.

** Johnson wins.

*** Lost reelection try.

the Republicans to tame inflation and provide a more sympathetic ear to business.

Republican Administrations, on the other hand, usually go too far in cutting government spending, fighting inflation, and tolerating unemployment and after awhile this leads to a deficiency in aggregate demand. Total consumer purchasing power cannot keep pace with the brisk expansion in capital investment. By the end of each Republican reign, supplies have mounted and we get a deep recession. It is then necessary to call the Democrats back to Washington so that they can expand consumer purchasing power.

Neither party can deviate very far from its underlying philosophy, no matter who is at the helm. Jimmy Carter, a southern Democrat from the center of his party, appeared to be well aware of the need to put out the fire of inflation when he took office in 1977. He proclaimed a strong anti-inflation stance, advocating deregulation and promising to balance the budget by 1981. However, a political party represents a particular constituency which will not let the leader veer too far from its basic economic approach. For this reason, Democrats are not good inflation fighters no matter what the party leader may profess. When Democratic leaders come eyeball to eyeball with the pain required to put out inflation, they are pressured by their constituency to back off.

On the flip side of the coin, when the economy is stagnating you can count on the Republicans, because of their constituency, to be too timid in applying fiscal stimulus. This was certainly the case in 1991-92 when George Bush backed off from giving a fizzling economy a dose of fiscal stimulus. In determining the direction of government policy, the party and its constituency is usually much more important than the man or woman who sits at its head.

There is a symbiotic relationship between the two political parties, wherein each one's strength offsets the other's weakness and this seems to work well for our political-economic system. Each party is a good half but an unlikely whole. The Democrats have been in the driver's seat in reforming and reshaping the nation and its economy so that it more nearly resembles the Democratic Ideal. They are committed to the humble members of society and have led the charge to empower vast groups of people so that they can get onto the playing field and become part of the great economic game. This has insured that prosperity is filtered down to the various levels of society and has provided a great deal of social mobility. It has expanded the market and improved the social and political life of the masses. However, when the Democratic party has been in control of the government for a while we get mounting taxes, rising living costs, and cheapened savings, along with rising social disorder. Inflation chokes off new investment and undermines the relationship between personal effort and personal wealth. It is necessary to call the Republican party back to power.

Republicans Bring Things Back to Earth

The Republicans play their part by bringing us back to reality after we have been out chasing rainbows. They recognize that a capitalist economy ultimately rests on its ability to increase capital—that is its stock of factories, equipment, and office buildings which are the edifice of an industrial economy. And to do so requires a climate that will nourish an entrepreneurial spirit so that large numbers of people are willing to commit their capital to these projects. In order to create such an environment, they provide incentives to business people and are willing, if need be, to put the economy through the wringer to stop inflation. Yet, after a long period of Republican rule there is a fall off in consumer purchasing power, a decline in social mobility as income inequality grows, and an unadventurous domestic policy wherein too few of the social cracks are fixed. You can bet that the Democrats will soon arrive in Washington and pursue a fresh approach to the economy.

There is an alternation of the political parties which seems to play into the Kondratieff cycle. The American political-economic system lurches to the left, then to the right, and once again back to the left, and each time the rules of the economic game change. Let us see how these pendulum swings between the two political parties help shape the Kondratieff wave.

• • • • • •

THE SHAPE OF AN UP WAVE

• • • • • •

The expansionary phase of a Kondratieff wave usually contains three stages which are separated by two serious contractions. These deep recessions scare large numbers of people and set off a crisis of confidence. They serve as small lessons of pain and help reduce the cost of capital and labor, thus laying the groundwork for another decade or so of sustained economic growth.

A serious contraction is accompanied by a severe fall off in industrial activity, a steep drop in business earnings, a sharp break in the stock market, and an extended decline in long-term interest rates. The fall off in industrial production and corporate earnings is usually deeper than during the two previous recessions. The telltale signs of a serious contraction are deep breaks in the stock market and long-term interest rates. Stock market prices and long-term interest rates provide a reading of people's mood. If the break in the stock market is the worst in at least a decade and long-term interest rates have experienced an extended decline, which lasts throughout the early part of the next business expansion, we can be sure that confidence is shaken and the trend of growing optimism has stalled. People shy away from economic commitments to some extent.

The severity of these contractions leads business people, consumers and investors to become a bit more cautious and increase their liquidity, that is, their cash on hand. Business managers reduce inventories, eliminate debt, and lay off workers. Consumers cut back their purchases and build up their savings. Investors scale down their stock holdings. Consequently, the cost of capital and labor comes down, and this will shore up profitability which, in turn, provides the underpinnings for the next stage of vigorous economic expansion, which usually lasts from about eight to eleven years.

As the next stage of the expansion unfolds, the serious contraction is still fresh in people's minds; business people, consumers, and investors remain cautious. Business spending for capital items increases only moderately. Consumers loosen their purse strings only gradually. It takes awhile before people eat up the reservoir of liquidity that had been acquired during the serious contraction and the economy develops speculative excesses once again. This stage of sustained economic growth is usually punctuated by one to three recessions, which are surprisingly mild. The fall off in industrial activity, stock prices and interest rates is normally well below that of the previous serious contraction. This is because business people have not exhausted their buying power. They are still quite liquid and able to take advantage of a moderate fall off in the cost of capital and labor to increase their spending for capital items.

Mild Recession Doesn't Serve as Caution

Later in the expansion stage, usually following one or two milder recessions, the pace of economic activity quickens. The experience of a rather mild recession, which was unable to stop the tide of rising profits, leads people to forget the serious contraction and lose their caution. People become bolder and spend the hoard of liquidity that was acquired during the last serious contraction. Business managers act recklessly, increasing inventories, capital expenditures, and debt beyond what would seem sensible. They become careless about costs. New businesses multiply and competition increases. The stock market surpasses its old high and attracts more and more participants willing to pay exceedingly high premiums to own stocks. Consumers dip into their savings and increase their spending. Simultaneously, workers, feeling less need to worry about their jobs, put less effort into their work, and productivity falls. The market for goods becomes saturated at the very time a rapid rise in business costs surpasses the ability of business managers to raise prices. Profit margins are strained and vigorous economic growth can no longer take place.

Chapter Eight

In order for another period of economic growth to occur, it is necessary to shake confidence so that business planners become more cautious and eliminate some of the waste and excesses that have arisen during this stage of sustained economic growth. A serious contraction will do the trick. It will curb some of the excessive optimism and prevent further misjudgments for a while again.

Serious recessions typically occur shortly before or after a new political party begins its reign. They serve as small lessons of pain and help foster a new mood which makes people receptive to a change in economic policies. Following

Table 8–1 Recessions During Expansionary Phases

Recession Begins	Industrial Production	Stock Market Break	Interest Rates Break (in mths.)
Jun 1899	10 percent	17 percent	25
Sep 1902	17 percent	31 percent	18
May 1907*	47 percent	42 percent	15
Jan 1910	8 percent	28 percent	6
Jan 1913	18 percent	23 percent	16
Sep 1918	19 percent	40 percent	2
Jan 1920*	30 percent	47 percent	28
May 1923	15 percent	18 percent	27
Oct 1926	6 percent	16 percent	16
Jul 1953	9 percent	13 percent	9
Aug 1957	12 percent	19 percent	18
Apr 1960*	7 percent	27 percent	40
Dec 1969	8 percent	36 percent	8
Nov 1973*	16 percent	45 percent	27
Jan 1980	13 percent	16 percent	3
Jul 1981	16 percent	24 percent	19
Jul 1990*	8 percent	21 percent	28

* Serious Contractions.

a period of conservative policies, there is renewed concern for the groups left behind and a rebirth of the liberal ideology. After the liberals have made a mess of things, the mood shifts to a desire to quiet things down and take a more conservative path.

Let us sketch the last two Kondratieff up waves, keeping in mind both serious contractions and the shifts in political parties. The first stage of the expansionary phase began in about 1897. The Republican party was at the helm. It put in place policies that helped generate a huge capital spending boom. Factories were running at full tilt and a buoyant investment climate prevailed. In order for the economy to begin a long wave up, it is necessary to save and invest so that we can build factories and buy equipment. The Republican party's approach to the economy enables this. This stage of the expansion lasted until 1907 and was punctuated by two fairly mild recessions which did not shake confidence. The rise in long-term interest rates was not interrupted for a period of more than 25 months. The first serious contraction of this up wave hit in 1907. Industrial production declined by about 30 percent, the Dow Jones Railroad Average, the leading average of that time, shed 42 percent from their peak values. In addition the rise in long-term interest rates was temporarily broken. Interest rates fell by 10 percent and the high made in 1907 held for six years.

This steep recession was the sign that the capital spending boom had gotten ahead of the consumer's ability to clear the shelves. A change in the direction of the economy was necessary. However, this did not happen immediately. The Republicans retained the White House in the election of 1908. Consequently, the economy couldn't pick up a head of steam and march confidently into the second stage of expansion. Early in 1910 the economy fell back into another recession which lasted 24 months. Although this recession was fairly mild (industrial production fell only 8 percent) it was the longest during an up wave.

We had to await the arrival of the Democrats before the economy would be able to accelerate again. They took over the reins of government in early 1913 and changed the government's focus to increasing consumer purchasing power. During the following seven years the tides of reform ran high as Woodrow Wilson pushed measure after measure of his New Freedom program through Congress. The economy experienced two more fairly mild recessions during the remainder of the second stage. The second of these, which began in 1918, was mostly due to the transformation from a wartime economy to a peace time economy. Interest rates hardly broke.

By early 1920 the wave of inflation had reached a spine-tingling 20.6 percent and was flooding the engine of economic growth. The economy came to a screeching halt and a deep recession, which some economists labeled a depression, began. Industrial production fell 30 percent, business profits evaporated into thin air, the stock market broke a whopping 47 percent, its worst break in more than 35 years and long-term interest rates fell 25 percent and this decline lasted 28 months which was their most extended fall since the turn of the century. With President Wilson incapacitated with a stroke, there was a crisis of confidence and the mood which had prevailed during the last eight years was broken. People had enough of reforms and crusades and decided to take things easy and enjoy themselves. The prices of American goods and services soared a staggering 52.5 percent during Wilson's second term, which proved to be the highest during any presidential term in this century.

1920's Bring Third Stage of Expansion

To begin a third stage of expansion, it was necessary to put out the fire of inflation and make investing tempting to risktakers once again. The voters turned the reins of government over to the Republicans. In early 1921, Warren Harding moved into the White House and brought with him a fresh approach to the economy which provided new incentives to save and invest. An eight-year period of solid economic growth, called the plateau period, followed. During the first four years inflation fizzled; it actually fell 5.5 percent. Social tensions eased and soon there was a renewed entrepreneurial zeal in business. By late 1927 the furious onward march of business had captured people's imaginations. The experience of two rather mild recessions, which were unable to stop the tide of rising profits led people to forget the serious contraction of 1920-21 and lose their caution. A spreading euphoria clouded the judgment of business managers, bankers, and investors. The prices of stocks were pushed to levels way beyond reason.

By 1929 the economy had again reached a point where the consumer could not keep pace with a whopping expansion in business capacity and it became apparent that a marked increase in income inequality between the rich and the other classes had developed. The economy was ready for another big spill, only this time because the whole economy was riddled with excesses the economy tumbled into a bona fide depression. The up wave of this Kondratieff cycle ended and we began a 20-year period of depression.

Another long expansionary phase began in 1949 and its three stages were quite similar to those a half-century earlier. Again the Republican party reached the White House during the first stage and put in place policies that would encourage a capital goods boom to take place. It was a time wherein jobs were plentiful, gasoline was cheap, and society was stable. Inflation which had averaged over 5 percent a year during the Truman years was running at only a tad above 1 percent during Eisenhower's reign. The powers that be didn't want to rock the boat. Although there were two recessions, both were mild. By the late 1950s the capital goods boom had gotten ahead of consumers' ability to increase their purchases. Also, following the unadventurous 1950s, the populace was becoming restless and ready for reform.

In 1960 another serious contraction began and the Democrats marched into the White House. This was the only serious contraction which did not have a big impact on industrial production and unemployment. In fact the brunt of it wasn't felt until 1962, when President Kennedy rolled back the price increase in steel and the business and financial community panicked. The liquidation, which occurred chiefly but not completely in the stock market, was resumed. The Dow Jones Industrial Average broke 27 percent, its worst break since 1938. Long-term interest rates also began a three-year slide and would not make new highs for almost six years. Enough people shed their optimism so that the conditions for a period of sustained economic expansion were now in place. People were now eager to strike out in a new direction both in dealing with the economy and in the social arena. The new administration applied the power of the federal government in an attempt to build a sustained national prosperity. Consumer demand exploded, industry expanded to meet that demand, and there was a remarkable eight-year period of economic growth. Unemployment, which had been at 6.7 percent when this period began, fell to 3.5 percent in 1968.

As in the time following the election of Woodrow Wilson a period of relentless reform began. The Democrats promised participation and entry to the good life to all groups. They pushed for civil rights, an end to poverty, and subsidized health care for the elderly, and thought they could rewrite the laws of economics to suit themselves.

Nixon Takes On Inflation

By 1968 the promises the Democrats had made to the public were becoming more and more burdensome and coming back to haunt them in the form of inflation. The election of 1968 was held against the backdrop of a nation that seemed to be ripping itself apart. The Vietnam War was producing social tensions on a frightening scale and inflation was running at an annual rate of 4.5 percent, its highest level in 16 years. The Republicans, with Richard Nixon at their head, reclaimed the White House. However, there was an important difference from the Republican restoration of 1920. This time the change in political parties came about without a parallel serious recession which would shift the nation's mood to accommodate a new approach to the economy.

The liberal tide of the 1960s was still running strong and people were not yet willing to tolerate the pain necessary to end the inflation. Besides, Nixon did not have a solid grip on government. In the election Nixon had garnered only 43.4 percent of the total vote, a mere $7/10$ of one percent more than his opponent, Hubert Humphrey. Nor did he have control of either house of Congress. Consequently, he couldn't allow the economy to fall into a deep pit so as to break the back of inflation. Instead, he applied only a moderate amount of restraint, which he called gradualism, to slow inflation and it failed. As a result, Nixon had a problem with inflation throughout his first term. In desperation, he instituted wage and price controls in late 1971. This threw a wrap over the economy and most people thought that inflation, which had fallen to a meager 2.8 percent annual rate in late 1972, was under control.

However, shortly after Nixon's reelection, inflation burst out into the open again and kept escalating. By late 1974 it was up and running at a more than 12 percent annual rate. This was the first time this happened during a Republican regime in this century. Finally, the Republicans got tough and put the brakes on the economy. Business turned down in late 1973. This time the administration was prepared to stay the course and not flinch as the bottom fell out of the economy. It was the deepest contraction since World War II. Industrial production fell 16 percent, the stock market plunged 46 percent, and long-term interest rates fell for 27 straight months and finally the mood of the nation changed. People were becoming more receptive to a conservative agenda.

However, this serious recession had come late in a Republican regime and therefore it was their policies rather than to those of the previous administration which were held responsible for the economic debacle. Also, Nixon's involvement in Watergate had left a bad taste in the mouths of much of the public toward the party of Lincoln. The result was that the Republicans were thrown out in 1976 just as a consensus was building to tame inflation and move in a more conservative direction. Yet, this same mood would make it difficult for a Democratic president to succeed.

The Democrats with Jimmy Carter in the saddle took over. Carter, the most conservative Democrat since Grover Cleveland, talked earnestly of taming inflation during the campaign. However, to stop inflation many must suffer and his constituency refused to give him this leeway and kept dragging him to the left. By 1978 inflation was back in high gear again, social tensions were mounting, and Carter had become prisoner to his own party. The demands of every group for their fair share of the resources and comforts had locked expenditures into an ever-rising, irreversible escalation. Once again the relationship between personal effort and personal reward was being eroded. Instead of presiding over a third stage of the expansion, the Democrats put us back into an inflation mode and we could not begin the plateau period. In 1980, inflation, which had been running at a moderate 5 to 5.5 percent annual rate when Carter took office, was in the stratosphere, escalating at a 14.7 percent annual rate and threatening to alter American life forever. During Carter's four years, America's prices rose 48.7 percent, the second worst performance during a presidential term in this century. No wonder Carter was defeated. This was the first time in this century that a political party, once attaining power, could not win reelection.

Chapter Eight

'80s Economy Flowers Like '20s

In early 1981, the Republicans returned to the White House and this time the public was prepared to go along with their program to bring down inflation and refuel the engine of American abundance. However, we still were to experience a pretty steep recession. In early 1981, the economy turned down into recession and unemployment reached 10 percent, its highest level since the great depression. However, the fall off in Gross National Product was less than in 1973-74, and the stock market fell only 25 percent, well short of the 46 percent break during the earlier serious contraction. 1981-82 was a deep setback, but fell short of being a serious contraction.

During the rest of the 1980s the economy flowered much like it had during the 1920s. Inflation went down for the count; by 1984 it was back down to an annual 4 percent rate and still falling. The economy sailed along, and new businesses were being created on an unprecedented scale. It was the roaring '80s.

A Kondratieff upswing usually unfolds in three stages. The first stage is generally presided over by the Republicans. Normally it is a capital goods boom accompanied by a great deal of social stability and a low rate of inflation. Next comes the stage of idealism and reform, which is typically engineered by the Democrats. During this period the government pushes programs to feed consumer purchasing power. This fuels a renewed burst of economic activity, and prosperity flows down to most levels of society. However, soon the beast of inflation is at the door again. There is generally one more stage with the Republican party usually calling the shots during that time period. This is a time of intense capital formation propelled by a resurgence of the entrepreneurial spirit. It is also a time when social tensions ease, and the rate of inflation subsides. This third stage of expansion is typically followed by the down phase of the Kondratieff wave.

In general, most shifts in political direction occur during or shortly after a serious contraction. These small lessons of pain discredit the previous approach to the economy and induce a change in mood so that people are receptive to an alternate approach to the economy. There were two times—in 1968 and in 1976—that a political change was out of step with the national mood and both of those administrations faced big problems. The two leaders ended their political careers in public humiliation before their prescribed time. Nixon was the first American president forced to resign and Jimmy Carter was the first president who was overthrown following a paltry one-term reign of his political party.

During the next chapter we will examine the retrenchment phase of the Kondratieff wave.

Chapter Nine
• • • • • •

THE DOWN WAVE
● ● ● ● ● ●

During a Kondratieff down phase there are typically two or three serious business contractions along with a wrenching collapse of the financial markets. Competition among business firms and nations intensifies. Many businesses disappear, while others fade into the background to play a lessor role in the American economy. Jobs evaporate, creating an army of unemployed and unhappy workers. Perhaps what is most frustrating about these times is the difficulty of getting back on the fast economic track. Solid economic growth cannot be sustained.

When business shows signs of life, hopes revive that the worst is over and the stock market, looking ahead to better times, experiences a huge rally. However, the business expansion sucks the wind out from the economy. A severe recession usually follows the expansion along with a steep break in the stock market which shatters the emerging hopes. Pessimism deepens, forming a dark cloud over the economy. Business people become even more reluctant to extend their economic commitments. As a result, the economy wallows around at the bottom unable to generate a head of steam and we are unable to put people back to work. At the same time the stock market seems stuck in the mire and does not experience a broad three-staged bull market. There is, however, one bright spot—falling interest rates.

During the last Kondratieff depression from 1929 to 1949, there were a couple of fairly vigorous business recoveries, but they did not lead to fast sustainable economic growth. For example, a cyclical business expansion began in 1933 and lasted about four years, but the weight of both a tottering debt structure and a contracting money supply made it very difficult for the economy to move forward. After a three year struggle, the economy showed signs of life in early 1936; more and more people felt we had turned the corner and the worst was over. However, they were mistaken. Despite very easy credit conditions, the number of new commercial loans remained abnormally low, competition remained ruthless and unemployment did not dip below 15 percent. Most importantly, individual purchasing power could not keep up with the pickup in production. So when business stepped up the tempo in late 1936 goods quickly piled up on the shelves. In 1937 recession hit with force: industrial production fell 31 percent, unemployment surged back over 20 percent and the Dow fell 49 percent. These events jolted confidence and during the following four years the economy and the stock market languished unable able to generate a full head of steam (see Table 9–1).

The current down phase will be the second slump of this 100 year cycle and therefore is likely to be much milder than the slump in the 1930s. Nevertheless, we are experiencing some of the very same problems that plagued us during the earlier period: difficulty creating jobs, reluctance to make commercial loans, difficulty in growing the money supply, increasing competition among nations, businesses and workers, and a weak debt structure all are eerily reminiscent of the 1930s. The similarities between the current slump and that of the 1930s suggest it is a good bet that before this slump is over we will see one or two more serious recessions, steep falls in the financial markets, further softness in real estate, and higher levels of unemployment. Also investors and business people probably will be caught off guard by a number of unpleasant surprises. Public frustration and pessimism will deepen and in all likelihood interest rates will continue on their downhill course. However, government props to purchasing power, such as unemployment insurance, social security and welfare, will keep the spending stream from drying up as it did in the 1930s. It seems safe to say that the Keynsian revolution—creator of government support

Table 9-1 Contractions During Down Wave

Recession Begins	Industrial Production	Stock Market Break	Interest Rate Break (mths)
August 1929	50 percent	89 percent	54
May 1937	31 percent	49 percent	55
February 1945	30 percent	23 percent	17
November 1948	8 percent	16 percent	17

of the economy—will prevent the type of deflationary collapse we experienced in the thirties.

In Japan the story could be very different. During the 1980s Japan built a bubble economy. Asset prices were stretched way beyond reason and the economy was leveraged to the hilt. Its manufacturing industries became the largest exporters to world markets. As other nations' economies experience low economic growth they are going to be unable or unwilling to absorb the products. Consequently, Japan's export industries will be left with severe over capacity. Because of this imbalance it is very likely Japan will have a particularly difficult time during the retrenchment period. It may well resemble a bona fide depression.

Down Wave Favors Democrats

The down phase of a cycle obviously favors the Democratic party. The severe weakness in the economy exposes the excess capacity built in during the up wave. Factories and businesses shut down meaning many workers lose their jobs. People turn to the government to protect jobs and to increase their purchasing power. In addition, people are more receptive to reform because the economy seems so bad. Democrats traditionally are better at addressing these desires than the Republicans. For example, in early 1933 the Democrats moved into the White House and stayed there for the remainder of that Kondratieff downswing. The serious contraction in 1937-38 did not open the White House doors to the Republicans. The 1930s were a time of very serious depression and a demoralized public was not about to put the economy back in the hands of the

Republican party, which was perceived to have "caused the problems in the first place."

Because the current down wave probably will not be nearly as severe as that of the 1930s, the Republicans may not be discredited to the extent they were 60 years ago. Consequently, the Republicans have a fair chance to play a political role during this retrenchment period. However, they will be operating against the historical forces and are not likely to stay in power as long as their reign in the 1980s.

Beside being fairly mild, this down phase also may be somewhat shorter than those in the past. Its length would compensate for the extended length of the last up wave, which lasted 41 years, restoring the rhythm of the Kondratieff cycle which in the past have lasted about 48 to 60 years.

In fact, we have a good chance of beginning the next up wave early in the 21st century. The next section will focus on developing a strategy to take advantage of the Kondratieff cycle.

Chapter Ten

• • • • • •

AN INVESTMENT STRATEGY

• • • • • •

The basic strategy for investing is obvious. Be bold and daring during a Kondratieff up wave. Be cautious and assume a defensive posture during the down wave.

Kondratieff up waves are times of rapid and sustained economic growth. There are glittering economic opportunities as economic development takes on a new direction, and investors find it easy to shake the money tree. Naturally during this period, it pays to take on risks. It is an ideal time to become an entrepreneur, to try for a better job, to buy real estate, to be as fully invested as possible in stocks, gold, and other investments. It is also a good time to go into debt because as interest rates rise over the years the rate you received will look ridiculously cheap.

For instance, people who borrowed long-term in the mid-1960s, say at 5 percent, would have been in the catbird seat in the late 1970s when rates were approaching 20 percent. Moreover, borrowers were paying off their loans in depreciated dollars.

Investment markets from the stock market to antiques, experience a powerful secular uptrend in prices during Kondratieff upswings. For example, the Dow Jones Industrial Average began at 161 in 1949 and reached 2999 by mid 1990—a gain of about 1,750 percent. (It has since risen to 3523 in early 1993). In the prior Kondratieff up wave, from 1896 to 1929, the Dow also rose by about 1,800 percent (see Figure 10–1). In the most recent up wave home prices went through the roof. In some areas of the country homes that sold for under $10,000 in the late 1940s, sold near $200,000 by the late 1980s. Other tangible goods tell the same story—price explosions of mammoth proportions. To be sure, the upward course of prices in investment markets is marred by setbacks from time to time. However, in an up wave these are not severe jolts; within a short period of time prices recover and reach new highs.

While stocks and real estate typically are outstanding investments throughout the whole of the Kondratieff upswing, gold and other inflation type hedges are not. The best time to own gold and other hard assets is during the first part of the Kondratieff upswing, which lasts until the plateau period. For instance, during the first phase of the last Kondratieff up wave, gold, which had languished at $35 an ounce until the late '60s, exploded to touch $850 in 1980—a mind boggling rise of 2,330 percent. The Dow Jones Commodities Futures Index went from about 37

Figure 10–1 Dow Jones Industrial Average 1900–1993

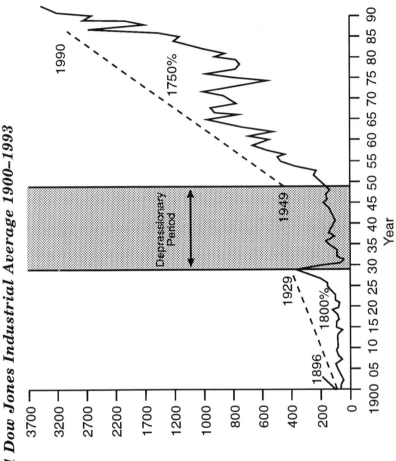

(adjusted) to 239—a rise of 545 percent. In fact, long-term bonds were the only investment that did poorly during this part of the upswing. They kept sinking as interest rates ratcheted upward. When the expansionary phase began in 1949, AAA Corporate Bond rates were at about 2.6 percent. They marched steadily upward until reaching 15.85 percent in September 1981 (see Figure 10–2).

During the plateau period things change a bit. Although stocks and real estate remain a good investment gold and hard assets do not. During the last plateau period from 1980 to 1990, gold fell from $850 to $283 an ounce. On the other hand, bonds typically experience a strong rise as interest rates tumble. During the 1980s long term bond returns almost kept pace with those on stocks and holders of 20-year zero coupon bonds and high yield debt did as well as equity investors and in some cases better.

It makes sense to cut back on investments as the plateau period lengthens so as to prepare for the down wave. An up wave usually ends about 7 to 10 years after the plateau period begins, as measured by the peak in long-term interest rates. Both of the past two up waves ended with a Republican administration in the White House, indicating we were serious about ending inflation and likely to go too far in curbing consumption.

Down waves are a treacherous time for investors. The economy will not get back on the fast track, and growth opportunities fade. Investors often face many unpleasant economic surprises; recessions are unexpectedly severe and accompanied by brutally severe unemployment. Business firms fight to keep market share, and the survival of many firms becomes increasingly uncertain. For example,

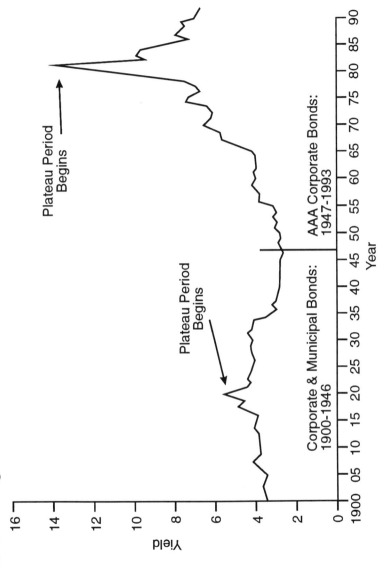

Figure 10–2 Long Term Bonds 1900–1993

during the last depressionary period two of the four economic contractions were very deep and prolonged. Industrial production fell more than 30 percent and
unemployment reached levels of more than 20 percent. In
contrast, the largest fall offs in industrial production in
the past Kondratieff upswing were merely 16 percent,
during the 1973-75 recession, and again during the 1981-
82 recession. Also, unemployment never went much above
10 percent.

Nearly every form of investment, from real estate to commodities, from stocks to antiques, tumble into a bottomless pit during a down wave. The foundation of these
markets, which were built during a time when prices were
on an upward slope, cracks, and profits that may have
taken a generation to build are lost, leaving a trail of
bewildered and shattered investors. Between 1929 and
1932 the stock market suffered a staggering loss of 89
percent. A $1,000 investment shrank to $110 in the course
of three years. Then, in 1937, just after investors had
caught their breath, the stock market went into another
sickening slump that did not end until the Dow had lost
52 percent of its value. In the 1930s the markets for real
estate, art, antiques, and other investments also suffered
chilling declines as buyers became scarce. Real estate, for
example, declined by more than 25 percent during this
period.

Investing During Down Wave

There is, however, one outstanding opportunity during a
down wave—high quality long-term bonds. Interest rates
stay on a downhill track throughout much of the down

wave, meaning the holder of long-term bonds is likely to earn more on his money than he would in any other investment. Given the treacherous environment for business, it makes sense to stick with the top notch corporations—businesses that are good bets to survive this turbulent period. In 1929 AAA Corporate Bond rates at about 4.80 percent began a lengthy retreat that did not end until they reached 2.46 percent in May 1946—a slide of almost 50 percent. During the 1930s, holders of long term bonds earned a return of nearly 100 percent, while owners of nearly every other type investment lost money.

After the heart of the depressionary period, opportunities begin to emerge, particularly in those investment markets that have been battered down to bargain levels. For instance, the Dow, after reaching a low of 98 in 1938, rebounded to 212 in 1946—a gain of more than 130 percent.

In general, a great deal of uncertainty characterizes down waves. People should be cautious and limit risks at this time. They should make sure their reserves are adequate to cope with emergencies that might arise, because emergencies will arise. Job uncertainty makes such periods emotionally trying. In addition, many of the giant companies of the previous 30 years face extreme difficulties; witness IBM, Sears, American Express, and Westinghouse to name a few of the household names of the past quarter century that were in deep trouble in 1992-93.

In general people should not borrow money to buy a home or start a business—at least until after the heart of the depressionary period. Homes, in all likelihood, will not produce the return they did during the up wave, which means renting will not be the losing strategy that it was during the expansionary phase. Remember, money normally increases in value during the down wave. It might be wise to postpone purchases as long as possible so as to take advantage of the fall in prices. It would not hurt to pay off credit cards, to increase disability insurance coverage, curb spending, and save, save, save.

Down waves generally end after the heart of the depressionary phase. The end is usually signaled by a turn up in both short- and long-term interest rates to a five-year high. For example, one year after the five-year high in 1948, a Kondratieff expansion began.

Up waves are a favorable time for investment. It is the time to create and increase wealth and take advantage of the many opportunities available. On the other hand, during the down wave, one should be prudent and preserve capital.

The next up wave is likely to begin sometime after the turn of the century. At that time there will be a chance to capture the fabulous returns that stocks, real estate, gold, and other assets provide. I will go into this in greater detail in the next four chapters.

THE END OF THE OIL AGE
● ● ● ● ● ●

The world is running out of oil. During the past five years, the amount of commercially recoverable reserves of petroleum has barely increased. And according to geological and seismic data, the prospects for big new discoveries are dim. The looming oil shortage is precipitating an energy crisis similar to the crises that occurred at the end of the three previous 100-year cycles. For example, at the end of the 17th century, England's forests were practically stripped of trees. The shortage of wood had become so acute that England lacked the charcoal needed for iron production. As a result, England could not produce the guns necessary for her military needs. The country had to put aside its centuries old fear of the toxicity of coal fumes and expand the production of coal.

Chapter Eleven

England again faced an energy crisis at the end of the 18th century. Although the country still had plenty of cheap coal, the new industries had taken up most of the suitable water power sites. In order to continue expanding, industries needed a mechanism to harness energy into mechanical energy that did not depend upon the location of the factory. Britain solved this problem by developing the steam engine, which helped lead the world into an age of industrialization.

At the end of the 19th century a threatening coal shortage appeared very menacing to contemporaries. People feared Britain's coal reserves would soon be exhausted. The government appointed a Royal Commission to study the problem. "There appears to be no reasonable prospect of any relief from a future of want in the main agent of industry. We must lose that which constitutes our peculiar energy," wrote W. Stanley Jevons, an eminent economist of the period in his book, *The Coal Question*.

Though Britain did not actually face a *shortage* of coal, it was rapidly depleting its cheap surface coal, meaning the cost of extracting coal would soar—and soar it did. As operators had to hire additional workers and plumb deeper shafts, the price of coal began to skyrocket. As coal costs mounted, new commercial ventures became too expensive to undertake. Fuel-saving inventions began to multiply, and there was a general search for alternatives. The problem was solved by the substitution of electric power, which used coal more efficiently, cutting costs.

Soon afterward, oil replaced coal as the chief source of fuel: because without cheap energy, there is no industrial payoff.

Why is there an energy problem at the end of each 100-year cycle? During the second Kondratieff upswing, vast new areas of the world industrialize, which leads to geometric increases in the consumption of energy. In the 1850s and '60s, Germany, France, and the United States began to industrialize. In the 1950s and 1960s Japan, South Korea, Brazil, and Taiwan began their takeoff into rapid economic growth. The world's demand for oil increased from just under four billion barrels in 1950 to over 20 billion barrels in 1973—a 7 percent compounded annual increase. Clearly this rate of growth in demand cannot be sustained indefinitely without outstripping finite world supplies. The fact is, given a consumption increase of a compounded 7 percent a year, had there been twice the amount of oil in the world it would have taken only eight more years to push the supply limit. An energy crisis late in the 100-year cycle appears to be unavoidable—at least until renewable sources of energy are developed.

New Energy Source Needed

Currently we face a problem similar to Britain's 100 years ago—the need to develop another plentiful and cheap source of energy in order to rev up the engine of industrialization once again. However, this time the problem is more serious because it is occurring in an economy that is also *structurally supply-constrained.*[1]

To understand the gravity of the current energy crisis, let's briefly run through the pertinent facts. During the 1950s and on through the 1960s, energy consumption and

---

1   This is a demand side economy (see Chapter 14) wherein it is difficult to generate large increases in the supply of goods.

the GDP (Gross Domestic Product) grew hand in hand, with approximately 1 percent energy growth needed to produce 1 percent real economic growth. However, as autos have become more fuel efficient, businesses have developed energy saving programs, and individuals have insulated their homes, this ratio has declined. There is much room for improvement, as we currently waste almost half the fuel we burn. We are in the process of redesigning every sort of machinery—from home appliances and autos to utility boilers and industrial equipment—to improve its energy efficiency. And we are showing impressive results. Already we are close to cutting in half the amount of energy needed for 1 percent of economic growth. According to some experts, we are on the way to bringing the rate of energy consumption needed to produce 1 percent of real economic growth down to .33 percent (one third of one percent). Nevertheless, if we hope to experience real economic growth of about 180 percent during the next 40 years, certainly more modest than the approximate 240 percent real growth during the past 40 years, energy consumption in the United States will increase by a minimum of 60 percent by 2030 (see Table 11–1). But where are we going to get the fuel necessary to meet the increase in energy consumption?

The conventional sources of energy—oil, gas, coal, and nuclear power—will not be able to meet the increased demand for energy. Oil and gas, supplied approximately 65 percent of our energy in 1990, down from 73 percent in 1980 and will decline even more. In fact, the most optimistic energy observers believe oil and gas will provide less than 55 percent of our projected needs by the year 2010 and keep on declining.

Table 11-1 Energy Consumption

Source	1960	1970	1980	1990	2010[b]	2030[b]
Oil	14.0[a]	29.5	34.0	33.5	31	25
Gas	6.0	22.0	20.5	19.5	19	18
Coal	13.0	12.5	15.5	19.0	28	33
Nuclear Power	0.0	0.1	2.5	6.0	10	18
Other (Solar, Fusion, Hydrogen)	1.0	2.5	3.5	3.5	7	36[c]
Total	34.0	66.5	76.0	81.5	95	130

[a] In Quads ; which is a quadrillion (1,000,000,000,000,000) BTUs. A BTU, is the amount of heat needed to raise the temperature of one pound of water one degree.
[b] Based on GDP growth of only about 50 percent to 2010 and 180 percent to 2030; an energy consumption / GDP ratio of .33 percent and optimistic assumptions for oil and gas consumption.
[c] To have another phase of industrialization, we are going to need a substantial increase in "Other" sources of energy; such as Solar, Fusion, Hydrogen etc.

Despite an abundant supply of coal, this power source has many drawbacks: deep mines are costly to develop, strip mining rips up the land, the resulting acid drainage renders streams biologically sterile, and coal miners strike at the drop of a hat. Not to mention that a massive expansion in the use of coal results in unacceptable levels of pollution. The enormous quantities of carbon dioxide emitted into the atmosphere threaten irreversible changes in the earth's climate.

Nuclear power, once considered the ultimate answer, also has little chance of answering the demand for energy. Public fear of nuclear power appears insurmountable. As a result, nuclear power companies face a long and costly process before they can get a plant into operation—an estimated 12 years, compared to about 1½ years in Japan. Furthermore, the available uranium resources will not support a large-scale nuclear program unless people are willing to use the costly and controversial fast breeder reactor.

Synthetic fuels, such as oil shale and oil and gas made from coal, also are not likely to solve the energy problem. They are very costly to produce, and unlikely to ever become cheap. Staggering amounts of capital are necessary to build conversion plants. Moreover, the conversion process uses a lot of energy and water, which is in short supply in those states that have the necessary shale and coal. Synthetic fuels are unlikely to amount to anything more than expensive temporary replacements.

Despite all the research being conducted on a variety of potential energy sources, including solar, geothermal, hydrogen, and nuclear fusion, these new energy sources still use nearly as much energy as they produce. They need lengthy further development before they become materially cheaper. The time necessary to increase their productivity is just too long to expect these new sources to meet our energy needs before about 2010. How are we going to bridge this transition period?

Look to Coal to Bridge the Gap

Until we come up with a new energy source, coal, despite all of its drawbacks, is the only realistic possibility. Oil and gas supplies are rapidly diminishing, and the obstacles to nuclear power are nearly insurmountable. The government appears committed to increasing the use of coal during the interim period in order to buy time to develop cleaner, non-fossil energy sources. As a result, coal will most likely provide about one-half of the new energy that will be needed between now and the year 2010. During this period, coal consumption in this country could increase by about 50 percent. Western coal fields, which produce an environmentally safer, lower sulfur grade of coal, are likely to provide most of the increase. The coal in this area can be gotten by strip mining, which has labor and safety advantages over underground mining.

But, if we are to have a full Kondratieff upswing, we must develop new energy sources that are environmentally safe and in large supply. Solar energy, nuclear fusion, and hydrogen are the most promising alternatives.

No other part of the energy spectrum has generated as much optimism and misinformation as solar energy. People hope that technology will be able to convert the sun's free radiation into a cheap and comparatively pollution-free source of inexhaustible energy. However, their hopes are unrealistic. Solar energy is not always available, which makes it an unreliable source of energy. Also, manufacturing the necessary equipment to produce solar energy uses a considerable amount of energy, which partly defeats its purpose of making more energy available. At the present, solar cells that convert the sun's energy directly into electricity cost nearly 40 times as much as conventional power sources that supply the same output—and it is unlikely these costs will decrease much in the foreseeable future.

Though scientists are still in the earliest stages of research on nuclear fusion, it promises a clean, practically inexhaustible, and safe form of energy. Nuclear fusion emits a lower level of radioactive waste products than nuclear fission, and there is virtually no possibility of a runaway chain reaction as there is with the fission process. However, fusion researchers are still trying to find a way to get more energy out of these machines than they put in. If the scientists are able to make the breakthrough, one cubic meter of sea water will provide enough deuterium to release the amount of energy equivalent to 2,000 barrels of crude oil.

Hydrogen, also appears promising as an alternative source of energy. but it too has its problems. Hydrogen can be derived by breaking down the molecules of water. It appears to be a clean, non-polluting, general purpose fuel, which can be used in transportation, as a source of heat, and to generate electricity in local power stations. However, we do not yet know how to store it in a safe manner. And, once this is solved, the even bigger problem of devising an inexpensive method of extracting hydrogen from water must be surmounted. At the present time the cost barriers to hydrogen are sky high.

Problem Is Cost, Not Technology

In general, technology most likely can surmount any barriers to the development of these new energy sources. The problem is cost. Like Britain at the end of the last century, we are not running out of energy. *Rather, we are running out of cheap energy.* Cheap fossil fuels made our current affluence possible, and until recently took very little work to obtain. Actually, one of the most impressive facts throughout the last 200 years was the increasing productivity of energy. We continued to find ways to use less energy in producing a unit of economic output.

Now that our cheap energy resources are on the verge of exhaustion, we will probably have to rely on energy sources that require an increasing amount of work and capital to obtain. Each of these new sources of energy, unlike oil and gas, require a number of additional processes after extraction, before they can be used, which makes them heavy users of energy. In short, it is possible no other energy source will be as cheap and efficient during the foreseeable future as oil was during its heyday. And this, of course, would mean that the next phase of industrialization will be more sluggish than the last two.

The immediate beneficiary of this looming oil shortage is likely to be the coal industry. During the down wave it might not be a bad idea to search out some of the leading companies tied to the coal industry. If the prices of these stocks experience a steep decline, they could prove to be bargains as this industry seems destined to play an important role into the beginning of the next century.

Another Kondratieff upswing will most likely generate significant increases in the demand for oil and its price will soar. At that point it will become apparent that the oil age is over. This will precipitate huge shifts in the prosperity of various industries and other sectors of the economy. Some businesses that had been quite successful will find their markets dwindling, while others will benefit as consumer's lifestyles undergo a drastic change. The most negative effect will, of course, be on the transportation industry, especially the automobile, which is very dependent on cheap oil.

It is estimated that automobiles, vans, and light trucks account for almost one-third of our total oil consumption in the U.S., and world-wide, autos consume almost one-fifth of every barrel of oil produced in the world. However, autos and other transportation designed for personal use, such as snowmobiles, motor boats, and light planes, are the lowest priority users of oil. They rank far behind food production, heating homes, running factories, or powering trains and buses. Energy for automobiles will take a back seat to higher priority uses, especially in the Third World countries which theoretically have the most room for auto growth.

Moreover, cars are costlier to drive than they were in the 1950s and 60s, and it appears they are going to become costlier yet as producers redesign automobiles to further increase gasoline mileage. It's a good bet that in the next century higher priced automobiles and increased gasoline prices will provide the incentive for an increasing number of people to seek alternative means of transportation.

As a growing public constituency for mass transportation and bikeways develops, restrictions on inner-city automobile travel will become more likely. Less money will probably be spent on street and highway building. This, of course, should make buses, bicycles and mopeds even more attractive. And we will see more acceptance of high mileage 'commuter cars' designed for shorter trips.

In Next Energy Crisis, Autos May Be Losers

If there is an energy crisis during the next century, autos appear to be the most visible loser. It is quite likely that after about 2010 automobile usage will increase at a much slower rate than it did between 1950-90—in fact, it may even decline. There will be fewer multiple car families, less teenage cruising, and people will keep their auto longer and drive it less. And there will be a change in lifestyles to one in which people are less dependent on the auto.

In the next century the world may begin moving away from an auto-centered transport system, and anything dependent on that system will be in jeopardy. Car dealerships, gas stations, motels, parking lots, drive-in banks, roadside restaurants, fast food places, suburban theaters, suppliers of automobiles such as the tire industry, auto parts firms, and stores and shopping centers located a long way from where people live and work will all feel the impact of reduced automobile travel. Recreational vehicles such as motor homes, snowmobiles, and motor boats should also suffer as the high cost of fuel dampens demand. Fewer people are likely to take long automobile trips, and this will probably affect the less popular vacation spots far away from population centers, although popular places such as Disneyland may still benefit from a novelty effect. Resorts which are hundreds of miles from metropolitan areas could be particularly hard hit. Many of these segments of an auto-centered society are likely to be left in the lurch by a new turn in industrialization.

The rest of the transport system—airlines, buses, trucks, and railroads—is likely to be reshaped by an increasing emphasis on efficiency, moving the largest number of people in the most efficient manner.

Huge shifts in living patterns are a likely outcome of the energy crisis. The migration from the cooler northern states to the sun belt regions, where less energy is used, should intensify. More people might opt to stay in the city rather than move to the suburbs. The downtown areas of many American cities will be reborn, and it's quite possible that property values in many of the outer suburbs will suffer. However, in some areas which develop suburban centers that cater to a wide variety of needs, such as in Los Angeles, suburbia will continue to prosper.

Some Winners at End of Oil Age

There will, of course, be industries which benefit from the end of the oil age. Mass transit companies will probably get added customers. More people are likely to own a small, fuel-efficient car for everyday use and rent a bigger one when they take a trip, and this may help car rental companies.

The de-emphasizing of the auto should help spur the growth of a home entertainment industry centered around video discs and tapes, along with cable TV, and provide the incentive for a family and home-oriented lifestyle. Those companies which supply instruments to regulate and control heat, appliances, and industrial equipment should do well. And micro-computers—the so called computer on a chip—which can control all kinds of things from auto engines to furnaces, will very likely play an ever-increasing role in the effort to conserve energy.

There may be a great deal of profit potential in identifying the longer-term move toward a new energy source and the restructuring of the economic base it should precipitate. Investors should remain alert to any new developments in energy that have become commercially applicable. We must remain cognizant of the fact that many, perhaps most, developments which seem to have a great deal of promise on the drawing boards never become commercially applicable. Some unforeseen problem crops up—such as high costs. The questions to keep asking are: "Have the breakthroughs already occurred?" And "Is this source cheap, plentiful and dependable?" By keeping these questions in mind, we may be able to spot a viable new energy source in its infancy. After that, investors should try to identify the key players within those industries. This will be especially pertinent after the turn of the century.

The energy picture casts a dark cloud over our future—especially for the next several decades. Not only must enormous quantities of new energy be developed, but there is a good chance we will also have to adjust to permanently higher energy costs.

Yet there is one area of the economy which shines through this cloud and promises to play an important role in surmounting the energy bind. That is the revolution of knowledge, which began in the 1950s.

THE REVOLUTION
IN KNOWLEDGE AND
COMMUNICATIONS
• • • • • •

The most striking development of the last third of this century has been the computer. Bank, brokerages, hospitals, airlines, to name a few, have adapted to the computer with breathtaking speed. It is impossible to go through a day without coming into contact with a process that has been speeded up, enlarged, or simplified by the computer. We are in the midst of a revolution in knowledge that is changing forever the way an entire nation works, plays, travels, and even thinks.

Chapter Twelve

Since the beginning of industrialization, there have been two other revolutionary developments similar to the present one. The first of these was the development of mass production of materials. The mass production of iron in the mid-18th century made iron cheaper, which meant it could be used in bridges, buildings and machinery. In fact, iron enabled industries to perfect production processes, thereby allowing business firms to produce for mass markets. This innovation was quickly followed by the mass production of cheap cotton textiles, propelling Britain into rapid industrialization in the late 18th century. By the 1830s, the mass production of materials had lost its force as a stimulus to rapid economic growth. Though gains in the production of other materials were still being made, they did not lead to a restructuring of the industrial base as did the growth of iron and cotton production.

Luckily, the second revolutionary development—the transportation revolution—had begun and was able to fuel the flickering fires of industrialization. The railroad defined the first phase of the transportation revolution. Railroad entrepreneurs built steel paths across nations, bringing new areas and new products into the market, lowering transportation costs, and adding a new dimension to the mobility of people and goods. As railroads pushed into virgin territory, new towns and industries arose in their wake, justifying the original enterprise. The industry's determination to build railroads before the demand for its services was in place gave force to this new development—the industry created its own markets, so to speak. Other developments in transportation also took place at about this time, such as the steamship, but the railroad revealed the benefits of technological progress as none of the others did. In the late 1890s, Alfred Marshall, the foremost British economist, remarked, "The dominant economic fact of our age is the development, not of manufacturing, but the transport industries."

By the beginning of the 20th century, the force of railroadization had moderated. The automobile became the prime impetus to rapid industrialization. It stimulated road construction, gasoline stations, roadside restaurants, suburban homes, to say nothing of the huge amounts of steel, rubber, and glass automobile production required. Like the railroad before it, it captured the imagination of people—it created its own markets. People rushed to buy autos before roads had been built. In fact, the popularity of autos stimulated the building of roads and auto-centered businesses, which in turn furthered the demand for autos. The automobile created a cultural revolution that reshaped society. By increasing mobility, the automobile pulled at the roots of the community and weakened the social threads that had bound people together. Victorian middle class values and attitudes gave way, family ties broke down, and a morality more attuned to the pleasure-seeking, alienated individual of the 20th century gained a foothold.

Technological Chain Reactions

Both the development of mass production of materials and the transportation revolution, began shortly after major depressions, and lasted approximately 100 years (see Figure 12–1). They provided business organizations with powerful new tools to adapt to an industrial world, offered exciting and "limitless" possibilities, and set off changes in people's attitudes and living habits.

151

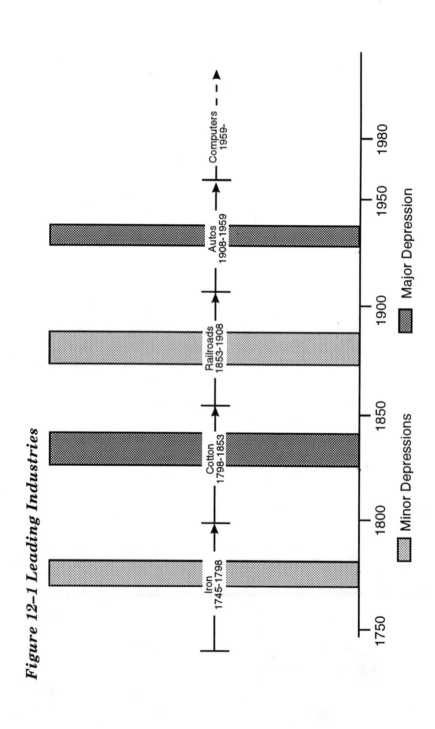

Figure 12-1 Leading Industries

Iron 1745-1798

Cotton 1798-1853

Railroads 1853-1908

Autos 1908-1959

Computers 1959-

1750   1800   1850   1900   1950   1980

Minor Depressions

Major Depression

The striking success of the first technological break-through in each of these revolutions revealed the possibilities inherent in the development, and led others to improve upon or extend its accomplishments. For instance, during the transportation revolution, the steamship followed the success of the railroad, only to be followed by the auto, the truck, the bus, the motorcycle, and the airplane in rather quick succession. Over a period of about 100 years we dramatically changed our mobility and restructured our economic system. In so doing we had, so to speak, solved an economic problem and were ready to strike out in a new direction. The forms of transportation that followed the auto, such as airplanes, helicopters, and rockets, no longer led to a vast restructuring of the economy, just as the materials that followed cotton, such as steel and chemicals, did not provide the impetus to change the direction of the economy. Instead the later developments played a supporting role to other innovations, helping to further refine the efficiency of existing business.

Newest Revolution—Computers

The third turn in the direction of industrialization has been the communications and information revolution which began in the 1950s with the computer. The speed at which the use of computers has spread is simply astonishing. Rapid technological advances have enabled manufacturers to pack more and more computing power into less and less space. The recent spearhead in the computer invasion of the American economy has been the micro-computer, the so-called computer on a chip, which packs the power of yesterday's large, expensive computers. These micro-computers are small, half the size of a fingernail, and are cheap to produce. They can fit into the corner of typewriters, cash registers, gas pumps, or be imbedded in machines, tools, and appliances. They are playing an important part in the trend to automation of both the factory and the office. Their role in energy conservation is substantial and still growing. They can be used in automobiles to regulate fuel use, adjust engine performance, and notify the driver on a dashboard when something goes wrong. In the home, they can turn off and on lights, control heat, and alert us when something needs repair. They can also be combined to provide incredibly cheap but powerful mini–micro computers which are invading our factories, offices, and homes. Future applications are virtually limitless and soon micro computers will become part of many things we make and use.

There are technological developments on the horizon that promise to make computers still smaller, more powerful, more versatile, and cheaper. These machines are being linked via telephone lines to banks, stores, government offices, central information terminals, neighbors' homes, and the work place. We are on our way to a global network of smart machines that can exchange rapid-fire bursts of information at unimaginable speeds.

Computers Helping Productivity and Profit

In both of the two preceding revolutions, the first phases began shortly after the major depression in the 100-year cycle. At this time, labor costs had risen due to the reforms in working conditions made during the slump, and these new revolutionary developments allowed business to become less labor-intensive, thereby enhancing efficiency.

The Revolution in Knowledge and Communications

The increased efficiency stimulated a sagging capital goods sector and permitted the economy to regain its lost vitality. The computer certainly resembles iron and the railroad in that it has allowed business to become more capital-intensive, and this is helping productivity and profitability.

The second phase in the prior two revolutions was based on accommodating consumer needs. Cotton and the auto were basically consumer goods. Interestingly, these two leading industries surfaced when the economy was being restructured around a new energy source. The cotton industry dominated when businesses were adapting to the steam engine. The auto became the leading industry when business was restructuring around electric power. Both cotton and the auto provided a tremendous psychological lift and helped spur a cultural revolution. Fashionable dress or fast personal transportation were no longer outside the means of most people, providing vast changes in the style of ordinary life. The automobile brought with it a feeling of mastery and power which enhanced people's self-esteem.

The outpouring of cheap, colorful cotton clothes in the 19th century brought in its wake a social revolution that was as meaningful as the one the auto fostered in the 20th century. The ordinary Britisher, who had been humbled by poverty, could now attain cotton products and inexpensive consumer goods, formerly available only to the rich. This provided an incentive to improve his status in the social order. The growth of middle-class consciousness, epitomized by the craving for a family-centered Victorian respectability and material well-being was to be the main feature of the 19th century landscape.

Chapter Twelve

If this pattern follows, the next phase of the knowledge and communications revolution will be geared to the consumer. Already, the improved capabilities and low cost of personal computers make them ideal for home use. Computers are able to compute income tax and keep supporting records, work out the family budget, keep tabs on investment portfolios, store a file of recipes, remind owners of upcoming appointments, serve as a smart typewriter, talk to your bank computer, call the fire department if smoke is detected in the house, or notify the police when an intruder is sensed, participate in conferences on specific subjects—from current affairs to gourmet cooking—or vote in a poll, of which the outcome can be reported instantaneously, and even play games with their users. Soon they will be able to plan a dinner with what food is in the refrigerator, get tips on supermarket sales or buy a suit or dress right off the screen. People will no longer need newspapers as such; both news and advertising will be fed directly into the living room. Mail volume will be cut drastically, because people will be able to communicate almost instantaneously by computer; and each family will have access to financial reports, educational materials, and the world's great libraries at their fingertips.

The home of the 21st century is likely to contain a family information, communications, and entertainment system with a mini-microcomputer as its nerve center. A home communications center is likely to radically change the way people spend their leisure hours. TV viewers will be able to call a number and request a movie of their choice, sporting events, concerts, or instructional tapes at whatever hour they wish to see them.

Advances Bringing Us Back Home

These new developments in the information age already have and will continue to dominate our lives and fundamentally change the world in which we live. They may help bring about a cultural revolution and alter life styles in a way quite different from the one sparked by the introduction of the auto at the beginning of this century. This cultural revolution may take us back into the home, renew interest in family life, and help rebuild a sense of community. If there is an energy shortage at the beginning of the next century, it will no doubt have an adverse impact on transportation and this will in all likelihood provide the incentive for people to adopt a lifestyle revolving around the home. Telecommunications will allow more people to work at home, shop by phone, and develop long-distance friendships with people miles and nations apart who share similar interests. Groups of people will be able to share an evening of interesting entertainment together. And as family members share in work and play, people will probably be drawn closer together.

The most exciting and profitable investment opportunities take place in the industries and companies on the forefront of the important revolution. These key industries proved to be such good investments that they became the basis for the popular business legends. During England's first cycle, it was the stories of those who made their fortunes in cotton—Robert Owen, Richard Arkwright, James Watt—that were continuously being retold. In the following cycle, the stories that dealt with laying the tracks of the Southern Pacific—or with the intrigues (involving Cornelius Vanderbilt, Jay Gould, Daniel Drew, and Jim Fisk) relating to the Erie Railroad—provided our business romance. Iron, steel, and coal came to assume places of importance, for they served as the material or fuel of the railroads. In the next cycle we got the auto, the story of Henry Ford, and the building of General Motors. Rubber and oil, by serving as automotive material and fuel, became important.

Currently, we meet up with the computer industry. As we all know, this has been the arena of spectacular growth during the last 35 years. The leading company, IBM, went from $3 a share in 1955 to $175 in 1987[1]—an almost 60-fold increase in 32 years. And scores of smaller computer companies tripled, quadrupled, and even experienced ten-fold increases in the span of a few short years.

But have we missed the boat? Have the stocks in the computer field already scored their spectacular gains? Fortunately for investors, Kondratieff downswings usually provide a marvelous opportunity to buy the leading companies in the key industries at bargain basement prices. While many of the smaller, under-capitalized companies are squeezed out during the retrenchment period, the leading companies generally come through in fairly good shape. The depression of the late 19th century was a good time to buy the leading, well-financed railroad companies, which were then selling at very low prices. And the depression of the 1930s was an outstanding time to buy the stocks of the leading auto companies, or, for that matter, some of their leading suppliers in the rubber and glass industries.

---

1   Adjusted prices.

Stocks Bought in Depression Brought Big Gains

General Motors, which could have been bought for $1.50 in the depths of the last depression, sold for $162 in the mid-50s—a more than 100-fold increase. During the same period of time, Chrysler went from $2 to $98, Goodrich from $3 to an unbelievable $530, Uniroyal (formerly U.S. Rubber) from $3 to $180, and Libby-Owens-Ford (the leading manufacturer of automotive glass) from $2 to $98.[2] Mouthwatering gains!

Anyone lucky enough to have invested $10,000 during the depression, spread among these five companies, might have realized about $1 million. Shorter time frames would also have yielded spectacular profits. For instance, by the late 1930s, when prosperity returned to the auto industry, General Motors sold for $38 a share and Chrysler reached $71—exceeding its 1929 high.

The reason a depression typically provides an ideal opportunity to buy these stocks is because the leading industry realizes unusually high profits and over-expands during the prior upswing, and as a result, suffers especially hard times during the slump.

However, this phase of the revolution does not end with the depression. Each phase lasts until the new Kondratieff upswing has begun (see Figure 12–1). For example, the railroad remained the dominant industry until about 1908, more than 10 years after the beginning of a new upswing. The auto then became the dominant industry and maintained its leadership until the late-1950s.

---

2   Adjusted prices.

Chapter Twelve

This down wave should, in all likelihood, present us with another chance to buy the stocks of the leading industry at bargain basement prices. The initial stage of the computer revolution was dominated by the large main-frame companies, IBM in particular. IBM today accounts for almost one half the revenues of the computer/data processing industry. However, recently the industry has been going through an important change. The more explosive growth is shifting to smaller computers—minis and micros, and these smaller computers cost far less than main-frame computers. They are within reach of hundreds of small business firms anxious to attain the productivity pay-off that these machines promise. Large organizations are using smaller machines to localize their computer operations rather than have them clustered in one computer center. This is known as distributed data processing. And as the performance of these smaller computers continues to improve and new applications are found, they will take an even larger share of the market.

This shift in the computer industry is similar to the one which took place in the auto industry during the 1920s. Ford, whose cheap, spartan Model-T had achieved phenomenal success during the first 20 years of the automobile age was slow to respond to the change in consumer taste which the affluence of the 20s presented. General Motors was building sportier, more luxurious, gadget-loaded cars, and overtook Ford. It became the number one company in the industry—a spot they have not relinquished to this day.

Currently we find IBM, which dominated the early stage of the computer revolution, with a bloated organization wedded to their past glories and slow to adapt to the recent changes within the industry, especially the move to the small computers. There are five other companies that have achieved important places in the industry and look like that they will be playing fairly significant roles for a while.

Digital Equipment is the leading manufacturer of network computer systems and has a stake in almost every segment of the computer industry. Its revenues are the second largest in the information processing industry. Hewlett-Packard is the second largest manufacturer of minis, with about 16 percent of the market. Hewlett-Packard is also a major designer and manufacturer of electronic testing and measuring equipment. Apple is the leading maker of personal computers.

The semiconductor industry, which makes micro computers, is no longer only a supplier to the computer industry, but has become part of the industry itself. Intel pioneered the microprocessor and is the largest manufacturer of integrated circuits. It has grown by leaps and bounds and appears to be the most innovative in the industry. In the software industry, Microsoft is the largest vendor of packaged software such as word processors and spreadsheets.

These six financially sound companies, which include IBM, are good bets to survive the retrenchment period and maintain an important presence in the industry. After they suffered a steep setback, it would certainly not be inconceivable to see gains in the price of their stocks somewhat comparable to those achieved by the railroads and auto after the last two Kondratieff downswings.

Chapter Twelve

Look to Up and Coming Companies

Looking ahead, past the retrenchment stage, the greatest opportunities will begin occurring in those companies that are on the forefront of the next phase of this revolution. However, rather than attempting to anticipate which companies will play the leading roles in the next thrust, we should let the market develop until the direction becomes clear. Remember that many of the early entrants in this field will drop by the wayside before the race is over.

Looking back at the automobile revolution, it did not become clear that Ford and General Motors were breaking away from the pack of hundreds of small automobile manufacturers and moving into positions of leadership until late 1908. It was in that year that Henry Ford introduced the Model-T—a light, inexpensive car that could take the family anywhere the largest most expensive cars were able to go. By 1911, Ford, which was producing about one half of the cars sold, had become the leader in that industry. General Motors, which had been put together in 1908 by combining a host of companies, including Buick, Olds, and Cadillac, was a distant second, with about 15 percent of the market.

In watching the development of the next phase of this knowledge revolution, sales figures and profits will tell the story, and these figures are usually fairly easy to get. When the trends become apparent, look for those companies which are emerging into positions of leadership—either number one, two, or three in the industry. Keep in mind, though, that a leading industry typically develops before the demand is overwhelming. Like the auto before it, there will be a growing desire to own a home communications system, which will stimulate a further building in the communications network, and this in turn will lead to further demand for home units. Investors should focus on those companies which are increasing their industry position—market share—or at least holding on to it. It would behoove serious investors to keep abreast of the trends in this important industry.

Investment Opportunities in Supportive Players

Another fairly reliable way to benefit from the next phase of this revolution is to look for those companies which appear to have the best chance of playing important supporting roles. Back at the turn of the century, it was obvious that rubber and oil would play an important role in the automobile revolution. And this provided investors with an easy way to profit from the revolution.

Now it seems certain that the information industry is destined to switch to fiber optics for the transmission of messages. In this new technology, which is many times more economical than electronics, impulses of light are transmitted along hair-thin strands of glass which are strong as steel.

Those companies making the machinery and equipment needed to splice silicones, the main components of microprocessors, have a promising future. The software industry, which provides the operating systems and applications for computers to function, is destined to play a major role during the next Kondratieff upswing. We can also predict with a fair degree of reliability that a vast array of information supplying vendors will spring up, and computer stores, where equipment will be sold, programming provided, and people taught to use the equipment, will multiply.

The knowledge revolution is still young and vigorous; the prior two revolutions lasted slightly more than 100 years. Yet, this revolution has not come a moment too soon. The expansion in man's muscle power, which generated our industrial progress, is in question due to the escalating price of energy. However, the multiplication of man's brain power through this new revolution may well enable industrial civilization to move forward in a less energy-intensive world.

Chapter Thirteen

• • • • • •

WHEN TO BUY AND SELL

● ● ● ● ● ●

BUY WHEN THE STREETS ARE RUNNING WITH BLOOD.

attributed to Baron Rothschild, about 1815

Generally, the best time to buy stocks is just after the market breaks an important prior low. "Blood will be running in the streets," as the saying goes. The outlook will be dismal, investors weary, and many respectable market commentators will be warning about the much lower prices yet to come. But stocks will be cheap and there will not be much risk in owning them.

Chapter Thirteen

In this atmosphere of fear and gloom, we can count on the fact that disillusioned investors will have liquidated their stocks. As a result, bad news no longer brings a rash of new selling. Nor is there a great deal of stock for sale overhanging the market. Thus, when bargain hunters emerge, eager to buy, the market recovers. And the economy improves as well. This is because the widespread pessimism caused businesses to dump inventories, reduce debt, and postpone capital expenditures. The reduced demand for funds leads to a steep tumble in interest rates, which in turn breathes new life into the economy. In addition, the dramatic cost-cutting campaign conducted by businesses provides a basis for raising earnings, fueling a long bull market in stocks.

Before I give a detailed explanation of when to buy and when to sell, a few words about how to distinguish a major bear market from its cousin, a bear trend. Any time the Dow Jones Industrial Average falls 16⅔ percent or more and reaches the lowest level in a year we can consider it a bear trend. In 1978, the Dow made a low of 744 which was 26 percent below the September 1976 high of 1014 and was the lowest price in three years. This was a bear trend. During a Kondratieff upswing, the low of the bear trend prior to the last bull market high is the important prior low because, when it is broken, it tells us that we are near the low of a major bear market.

For example, the stock market experienced a bear trend in 1960. The Dow Jones Industrial Average fell more than 16⅔ percent from its all-time high of 685 to 566, which was lower than any price since December 1958 or the lowest price in 22 months. Following this bear trend, the

Table 13-1 Major Buying Opportunities

Buy	Price	Time and Percent before Bottom	Percent below last Sell Price	Sell	Price	Percent from Absolute Top	Gain/ Loss
Aug. 7, 1896[a]	28.7	1 day 1%		Aug. 11, 1905	82.2	25%	186%
Oct. 22, 1907[a]	59.1	20 day 10%	28%	Oct. 20, 1919	158.0[b]	3%	168%
June 20, 1921	64.9	9 week 1%	43%	Jan. 31, 1929	317.5	20%	401%
July 8, 1932[c]	41.2	(same day)	87%	Aug. 8, 1936	169.1	15%	312%
Apr. 14, 1942	97.9	10 day 5%	42%	May 28, 1946	211.7	0%	116%
June 13, 1949	161.6	(same day)	24%	Dec. 23, 1958	566.4	30%	250%
June 14, 1962	563.0	8 day 5%	1%	Nov. 10, 1972	995.3	5%	77%
Dec. 13, 1974[c]	592.8	1 wk after 3%	40%	Aug. 24, 1989	2734.0	28%[d]	361%
Average		3%	38%			16%	234%

a Based on the railroads, which were the leading sector at the turn of the century.

b The approximate value of the old Dow Jones Industrial Average, which was discontinued in late 1914. The new Dow was 109.1.

c Following take out of a 5-year low.

d As of May 1993.

Chapter Thirteen

Dow rallied and made a new high reaching 734 in November 1961. From that level the Dow plummeted and on June 14, 1962 closed at 563 which was lower than the 1960 low of 566. This was a major bear market and left many investors bloodied (see Figure 13–1). Major bear markets, unlike bear trends, take out an important prior low.

While major bear markets during the upswing are typically a one-stage affair, this is not so during the down phase of the cycle. The generally weak financial conditions make it unlikely that the Dow will rally back and make a new high following a bear trend. In this case, all that is required to set up a major bear market is a rally to the highest price in a year and then a break to below the bottom of the previous bear trend. For example, after the Dow made a 15-year high at 212 in May of 1946, it fell to 163 in October of that year and that low was the lowest price in more than a year. From that level the Dow rallied to 193 in June of 1948 which was the highest price in more than a year. When the Dow fell and broke the low of 163 in June of 1949 an important prior low was broken (see Figure 13–2). This major bear market was a two-stage affair, as they often are during the down phase of the cycle. In addition, at the beginning of the depressionary phase it appears that for a bear trend to be an important prior low, it must also be a five-year low or more. Remember that you are letting the air out of a 30-year or more rise in prices at this time. If at the beginning of the retrenchment phase, the prior low that is broken is not a five-year low, there is a good chance we are not near a the low of a major bear market.

A buying opportunity occurs shortly after the break of the important prior low. It is the time to disregard the prevailing

Figure 13-1 Dow Jones Industrial Average 1958–1975

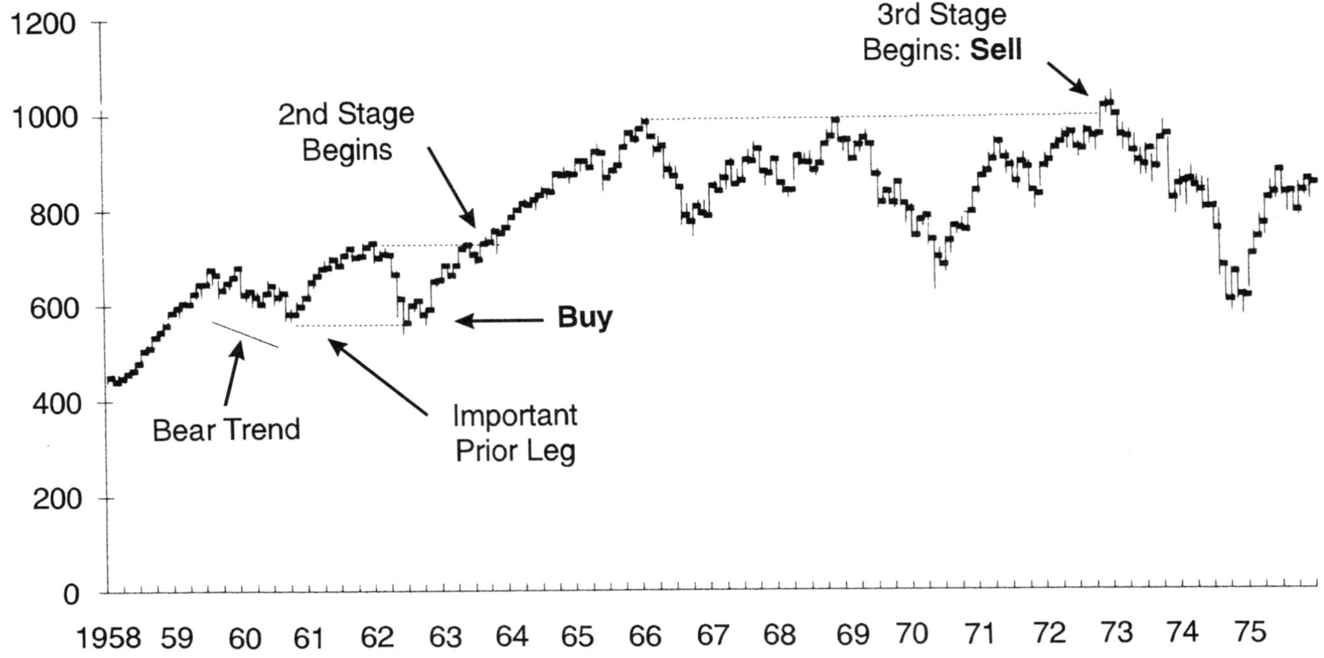

3rd Stage
Begins: **Sell**

2nd Stage
Begins

Buy

Important
Prior Leg

Bear Trend

1200 1000 800 600 400 200 0

1958 59 60 61 62 63 64 65 66 67 68 69 70 71 72 73 74 75

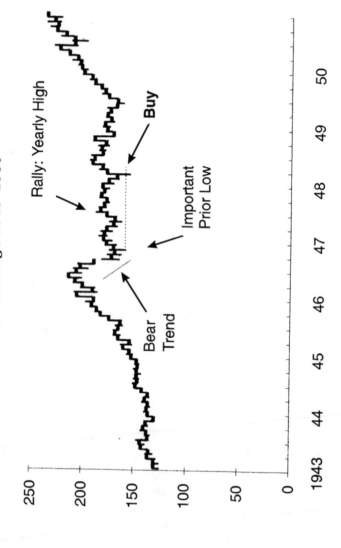

Figure 13-2 Dow Jones Industrial Average 1943–1950

pessimism and buy stocks aggressively. If the prior low that is broken is a five-year low, you can expect even more pessimism to follow. In this case investors could wait about three months before buying. Since 1896 the Dow Jones Averages broke an important prior low eight times and each time a bottom was made shortly thereafter. For example, the Dow made a bottom at 535 on June 28th 1962 just eight trading days after and 5 percent below the day of breaking the 1960 low. From that point a major bull market began, which was to last more than 10 years and take the Dow up to 1051. There were eight buying opportunities beginning with 1896 (the start of the last cycle) and including those in 1907, 1921, 1932, 1942, 1949, 1962, and 1974. All occurred within nine weeks and an average of 3 percent above the absolute bottom in the stock market (Table 13–1). Following each of these bottoms, a major bull market in stocks began and lasted anywhere from four to as long as eighteen years.

Trick in Knowing When to Sell

It is a bit trickier to determine when to sell. This is because the subsequent bull markets differ depending upon whether they are occurring during the up phase of the Kondratieff cycle or the down phase. During Kondratieff up waves, a psychology of increasing optimism leads people to extend their economic commitments. The result is a series of broad, three-staged bull markets, each of which continue on up until investors become over-optimistic. These secular bull markets generally last at least eight years and sometimes a great deal longer (see Figure 10–1).

The first stage of a broad bull market is the recovery. It lasts until the Dow has made new all-time highs. During this stage the public is still influenced by the recent bad times. People are skeptical and the market in general is under-priced. As a result, there are many good values. Once the Dow Jones Industrial Average makes a new all-time high the second stage begins. This breakout induces a major change in perceptions. There is a shift of investor sentiment. More people recognize and focus on the favorable economic prospects and the speculative juices begin to flow. A significant number of new risk takers are attracted to the stock market and line up to buy stocks. This creates a vast reservoir of buying power, which provides an underpinning to the stock market, and as a result, we can generally count on the bull market to last a minimum of a little more than four years, say 49 months from this point.

Sometime during the second stage the Dow experiences a break of 16⅔ percent or more. This break does not have to make a yearly low. It is the first important setback since the new high, and shakes up a lot of the new investors. However, it is by no means the end of the broad bull market. Too many people still believe the stock market is a good place to be and are willing to buy the break. Typically we can depend on a return to new highs.

Once the Dow returns to new all-time highs following this setback, the third and last stage begins. During this stage a spreading euphoria colors people's perceptions. They think we are on the brink of perpetual prosperity. They throw caution to the wind and bid up the prices of unseasoned stocks to ridiculous heights because they expect improving business conditions will justify such prices. Once we are into the third stage and 49 months have passed since the beginning of the second stage, investors should think of selling. They should be looking for clues to an impending top. Watch for a great deal of optimism and speculative activity in both the stock market and the economy.

To prove my point let's look at the bull market that followed the bear market of 1962. The Dow recovered and made a new all-time high in September 1963, marking the beginning of the second stage. This meant we could expect at least about 49 months of fairly clear sailing. The first break of 16⅔ came in August of 1966, about 35 months into the second stage. However the market had difficulty making a new all-time high. Following a try which lasted until late 1968 the Dow faltered and made a new low in 1970. It was not until November of 1972 that the Dow took out its 1966 high of 995 (see Figure 13–1). This was the time to think about selling. Two months later and about 5 percent higher the Dow made its top.

Bull Markets in Depressionary Phases

Contrary to what many people may believe, bull markets occur during the depressionary phase. However, the prevailing pessimism, wherein people are not willing to extend economic commitments, keeps them from becoming broad, three-staged affairs. Nevertheless, it seems investors can wait about 49 months from the absolute low before selling. If the Dow has reached at least a five-year high by this time investors should think of selling. They should be on the lookout for a market top.

Investors who sold when the marks set out above were reached, received approximately 16 percent from the high water mark on average. In addition, each of the eight sells came before market tops by anywhere from one day to as much as three and a half years. Even though several bull markets still had a way to go—four gained an additional 20 percent or more from this point—these signals did a credible job of getting investors out fairly near the top. In fact, six sells were within seven months of the actual top. At the very least, investors should consider trimming their portfolios at these signals, and when they see more concrete signs of trouble on the horizon they should dump the rest.

On the other hand, anyone who bought after these points were touched would have been very disappointed. Following the last seven bull markets, there were five major bear markets wherein the Dow fell 40 percent or more. In the two other major bear markets the Dow fell by more than 25 percent (see Table 13–1). When these points are reached, investors usually hear many optimistic predictions for higher levels in the future. For instance, in January of 1973, just as the Dow was making a final top, *Barron's* printed the conclusions of its annual year-end panel, consisting of ten stock market experts, under the heading "Not a Bear among Them." Their modest expectation for 1973 was 1200 on the Dow. Over-confidence causes people to view the market through rose-colored glasses. Investors are likely to be told that the old rules no longer work, and this time "things are different." They should ignore that advice.

Invariably the situation is not as favorable as the experts are painting it. Just as too much pessimism establishes the conditions for a significant improvement in business along with a long rise in the value of assets, over-optimism sets up the conditions for a serious contraction along with a severe break in the stock market. Optimism causes people to act in a way that has an unfavorable long-term effect on profitably and performance. For instance, business people are likely to increase inventories, take on more debt, add workers, and begin new capital projects. A mushrooming demand for credit drives interest rates through the roof, which in turn puts a noose-like grip on the economy and sets it up for a serious contraction. In addition, you can count on a whopping increase in the cost of doing business, resulting from the increased interest rates, to soon produce a spate of dismal earning reports. Every period of over-optimism has been followed by a serious recession and a major bear market in stocks.

After investors have sold out, they should wait for the next major bear market before buying. During the expansionary phase investors may not want to get out of stocks completely. They may want to keep a small commitment just in case a major bear market does not occur. If so, these positions should, of course, be in stocks the investor thinks will resist a bear market.

Using the signals sketched above, since 1896 we had eight "buys" and "sells." Each was very profitable, with returns from 77 percent to 401 percent and an average gain of 234 percent before dividends. Perhaps more importantly, during each of the seven major bear markets investors would have been out of the market and saving on average 38 percent and as much as 87 percent in 1929-32. Each time, after selling out, the investor would have been able to buy back lower (see Table 13–1).

Chapter Thirteen

Beware of Over-Optimism

The last sell suggested by these indicators came more than three years ago. Although stock prices are higher today in early 1993, it is quite likely that sometime before the turn of the century recent buyers, say those who joined when the Dow was over 3000, will wake up with egg on their faces. Once again people believe the stock market is a game without losers. More and more people are marching into the nation's brokerage houses chanting the mantra, "the stock market is the best investment around." If you are down for a one-year period that's no matter, wait for five years. If over a five-year period you are still a loser, no sweat, wait for twenty. We have almost 100 years of stock market history to show that in all twenty-year periods investors in stocks come out ahead. The current gospel has helped propel stocks beyond all reasonable standards of value. As of this writing, stock prices are seriously overvalued, more so than in any period in the past, and we are at the beginning of the down wave of the Kondratieff cycle. If the past is any guide to the future, we can expect to see a series of major bear markets, during which there is a good chance the Dow will sink to at least 1700, which is approximately 38 percent below the last sell suggested by the indicators.

Early in the next century when we experience another up wave, the stock market may have a series of broad bull markets and the Dow may well surpass the 10,000 marker. But that is a different story. Now, let us turn our attention to inflation and how it is changing the Kondratieff cycle.

THE AGE OF INFLATION: THE CHANGING NATURE OF THE KONDRATIEFF CYCLE

• • • • • •

Prior to the late 1930s, the Kondratieff cycle operated within the environment of a laissez-faire economy. The economic revolution inspired by Keynes altered the balance between spending and savings, and this change has affected the way the Kondratieff cycle works.

Prior to the 1930s governments restricted their role in the economy. They did not attempt to prop up purchasing power. The only acceptable government intrusion into the economy was to provide a stable monetary framework to induce people to save. Savings, according to economists of that time, were the key to material progress. They would be channeled into productive investment, and this in turn would lead to a vast expansion in the supply of goods. As a result, pre-Keynesian economies did not have trouble attaining extraordinary increases in output. Economists of the period did not question the economy's ability to generate rapid growth in the supply of goods.

However, there was a problem. Every so often the productive capacity outstripped people's ability to consume and it became necessary to eliminate the excess capacity that had developed. This instability vented itself in long, sickening depressions. The problem, as Keynes explained it, was a deficiency of demand, which at times could throttle the engine of economic growth and produce a nightmare of unemployment. To correct this malfunction, Keynes insisted that a government should pump up purchasing power through tax cuts, heavy spending, and the outright creation of money, and this would keep the economy on a growth path.

Today, governments throughout the Western world stimulate purchasing power, via unemployment insurance, Social Security, welfare, and cheap credit to home buyers. These policies encourage a huge shift of money and credit from savings into consumption. Yet, this also this hinders the capital formation process. Less money is available for new investment in plant and equipment and consequently, it becomes increasingly difficult to generate the supply growth necessary to accommodate the swelling demand. The result: the nation's spending power periodically overwhelms its productive capacity—the mirror image of the problem faced in a pre-Keynesian economy—and this sets off a feverish and protracted inflation, such as that in the 1970s.

At any given period, a nation's economy displays a structural bias either to the supply side or the demand side. Solutions meant to eliminate the bias may be successful, but they change the structure of the economy and create a bias in the opposite direction. In the 19th century, the government focused on the supply side, and as a result, productive capacity grew faster than spending power. This made for deep and prolonged depressions and *there was a tendency for prices to fall*. When the government shifted its priorities to the demand side, the nations spending power grows faster than its output and *prices must rise*. Simple Economics 101.

Keynesian Legacy—Bias toward Inflation

We are left with a structural bias toward inflation. Since the early 1940s prices have been in a continuing and protracted rise, in sharp contrast to the previous century when the pattern of prices was a 100 year downward slope. This is exactly what theory would dictate.

By the late 1970s people began to realize that the unwanted and unforeseen outcome of Keynesian economics was a propensity toward inflation, along with economic stagnation. In 1980 Ronald Reagan arrived on the scene with a program to revitalize the productive power of the nation. He sought to do this by getting the government out of the economy and reimposing the incentives of the marketplace. Essentially, Reaganomics was a noble attempt to return to good old laissez-faire capitalism.

But they could not turn back the clock. The world in which laissez-faire economics flourished has passed. The 1930s were a major turning point in Western society. There has been an irreversible shift in attitude. People recognized that by handing the reins of the economy to government, they could have a new type of capitalism: capitalism with a heart, capitalism that brings with it the promise of economic stability and social justice. People are no longer willing to suffer the hard times which often result from a cruel and impersonal marketplace. A faith in free markets was replaced by the belief the government can and should steer the economy to the land of limitless abundance. Since the 1930s, any presidential candidate, whether Democrat or Republican, has had to promise prosperity if he hoped to reach the White House. If that promise is broken, the voters will show no mercy at re-election time.

Flaws in Reganomics

The flirtation with Reaganomics was not based on a reacquired faith in free markets. Reaganomics was able to capture the imagination of the American public because the Administration presented it as virtually painless therapy. Ronald Reagan promised an easy transition from an inflationary to a noninflationary economy. However before long Americans saw that the price of attempting to resurrect a supply-side economy was sending millions of workers to unemployment lines. In 1992, Americans rejected that solution to inflation and sent the Republicans packing. Bill Clinton and the Democrats took over and, once more, the government is taking an active role in stimulating the economy. Structural shifts in the economy, such as the change to the demand side in the 1930s and 1940s, are *not* easily undone and most attempts to backpedal are doomed. Make no mistake about it—we will remain in this demand type economic structure for a long, long time to come.

The Keynesian revolution was no accident. Actually it is part of an approximate 300- to 400-year cycle first described by the Belgian historian, Henri Pirenne, that goes from economic freedom to economic regulation and back again. It can be traced all the way back to the first flickering of commercial activity at the dawn of the 11th century, when the Western world awoke from the Dark Ages and began to cast aside a feudal system that kept most people in bondage.

As we begin our story in about 1000 A. D., there were no troubling restrictive regulations on commerce. An increasing intensity in economic activity furnished men with a new means of existence and aroused the hope of gain. There was an uninterrupted migration of peasants from the countryside to towns where developing marketplaces furnished regular occupations. After a year and a day spent in a town, a peasant became legally free to join in a vibrant new merchant class. Trade grew, the standard of living rose and the first fortunes in moveable property, since the decline of the old Roman Empire were acquired. To be sure, the commercial activity involved simple operations, but soon some of the trading towns took on an industrial flavor and developed an export industry, such as cloth.

Chapter Fourteen

By the early 13th century many of the towns had become an economic jungle. The merchant class had grown tremendously, and as a result, competition had become cutthroat. A new materialistic spirit had taken hold. There were many complaints that the new bourgeoisie class were abusing their power, and no governing authority existed to protect the poor and the powerless.

Protectionism Stifles Free Economy

In about the mid-thirteenth century 200 years of free capitalistic expansion came to an end, as almost every town sheltered itself behind the ramparts of protectionism. They began levying taxes, fixing wages, prohibiting innovations in tools and techniques, and regulating the conditions of work, all of which severely limited the independence of the merchant in commercial matters. At the same time the church stepped forward and forbid both the lending of money at interest and all profits exceeding a just price. These regulations held competition in check, and sought to defend the community from the encroaching commercialism and its abuses. But they also blocked entry into the bourgeoisie class and some of the personal freedoms linked to a free economy were also lost.

Although industrial and commercial advances slowed, the standard of living continued to show impressive gains for a while. The prior period had left as its legacy a large reservoir of wealth, and consequently, when the governing authorities stabilized commerce and directed a more even distribution of goods, the prosperity spread. However, after about half a century or so, bottlenecks appeared and a process of economic decline ensued. The authorities debauched the coinage, which led to inflation and wild price fluctuations. A spectacular series of bankruptcies brought down a majority of the large banks. Some trading centers disappeared. Yet, some men of enterprise were able to surmount the obstacles during this long period of economic decline and attain wealth and status. But they accomplished this largely through a shift in the ownership of the already existing wealth, (i. e., mostly through banking, brokerage, and middle-man type operations; credit, for the first time, was used on a large scale) not by adding to the productive wealth.

Nevertheless, by the early 14th century the retardation of commercial activity had induced a shift in mood to one of deepening pessimism. People felt prosperity would never return. And for a long while they were right. During the following century war, plague, famine, and social rebellions based on the belief that every man should have as much as the other brought European society to its knees. It was a dark century of economic depression, falling population, widespread misery, destruction and a breakdown of authority. The traditional religious values no longer held sway, the fleshpots were kept boiling and people joined in the "Danse Macabre," the cult of death.

Monarchies Set Commerce Free

Early in the fifteenth century the great monarchies began to form. They subjected the towns to their superior power and set commerce and industry free. They did away with limits on speculation, abolished the fetters on commerce, and put a stop to the meddling of authority in relations between employer and employed. Energies were refreshed and there was a great expansion in trade. New industries appeared. Enormous new fortunes were built. Their was a new fluidity in social relations as the door to social mobility opened once again. The new merchant class was larger than the one before. It had more opportunities for free choice and personal initiative, and it firmly believed, "liberty was the soul of commerce."

This was a time of great cultural achievements and comparative stability. A Protestant revolution recharged the batteries of religion and inspired people to value diligence, thrift, and temperance, fortifying the "spirit of capitalism."

By the mid-16th century this phase of capitalism reached its zenith though most contemporaries could not have realized it at the time. Competition had gotten out of control. The new rich had become very powerful and were abusing their privileges. A century of whirlwind change had left many people breathless. The current of commerce was ready to change direction once again.

Soon nearly every state sealed off its markets to imports and attempted to increase the production of their local industries. The object: to induce the balance of trade in their favor. These policies, now known as "mercantilism," put a stop to the ruthless competition of the early 1550s. But they also helped fuel a great inflation that was to last for nearly a century.

Yet output did not fall immediately. The fact is that governing authorities, when they impose their will on commerce and industry, usually do so in two steps. The first step is hesitant and leaves much of the prior economic structure in place. As a result, when the various governments move to aid the less fortunate, a greater share of the wealth flows to the lower strata of society and creates a demand stimulus that gives new life to the economy, and the standard of living continues to show impressive gains. This is a transitional period which usually occurs following the first move from a free market economy to a period of government intervention. However, after about a half of a century there is a noticeable deceleration in output. This was the case in the early 17th century, when a budding pre-industrial revolution in both England and France ground to a halt.

Social Order Breaks Down

In the 1620s the Western European economies collapsed, and a brutal and ongoing 30-year war traumatized Europe. Widespread misery and discontent precipitated a crisis that shook Western Europe at its roots. Order broke down as rebellions in community after community flared up. During this time the growth in population leveled off. An onslaught of worldly materialistic values, such as avarice, consumption, hedonism, and self-expression weakened the older traditional religious values and helped undermine the authority of established institutions.

In response, the monarchies extended their control until it was nearly absolute, usurping many of the political rights granted during the Renaissance. At the same time, following the lead of Colbert in France, governments pushed mercantilism to its extreme. The nation-states introduced comprehensive codes to regulate production and trade, and this prevented anything from changing. To help keep order and administer the complex economic codes states put in place vast bureaucracies staffed by a multitude of "courtiers" and "officers." Membership within these agencies guaranteed wealth and status. Though others also acquired riches, it was mostly those who were more adept at rearranging, rather than increasing, the existing wealth. Under the added weight of an inefficient and parasitic bureaucracy, commerce continued to shrivel and trade stagnated. Real incomes did, in fact, fall for the first time in more than 200 years. Finally, in the late 17th century, a sense of hopelessness that economic life would get any better, along with a revulsion to the free-spending and loose living habits that had taken hold, produced a Puritan revolution in England.

In the mid-eighteenth century Britain relaxed some of its strict mercantilist restrictions, breaking ranks with the rest of Western Europe. An unanticipated but pleasant step up in production along with a decline in prices followed. Though the expansion was limited because many restrictions remained, the possibilities of a free market economy could be seen. A constituency that advocated lifting all the economic controls began to form. But it was too controversial at the time.

Laissez-Faire Makes Comeback

When in the early 19th century a depression of awesome proportions struck, those who had advocated removing all the restrictions aquired credibility. In the early 1840s, England finished the job and removed the remaining restrictions, and the economy soared. A period of wealth creation followed, the likes of which the world had never seen. People from all walks of life became believers in a laissez-faire economy. Over the course of the century, millions of men and tens of thousands of women, born without privilege, joined the middle class. As governments loosened their political controls an enormous expansion of the boundaries of freedom and choice also followed.

Yet people carried their faith in a free market to an extreme. A glaring contrast between the rich and poor developed, and many suffered the abuses of the new freedoms. Again a movement to protect the underclass developed. These critics of the free market, many of whom frequented London's intellectual gathering places or lived in New York's Greenwich Village, claimed the free market fostered unbridled competition that set not only business firms, but nations and individuals at economic war with each other, perpetuated grave inequities of wealth and extravagant rewards for success, and as a result of the continuous and accelerating technological and social change, people were in a constant state of psychological shock. Their prescription? Why of course—the re-imposition of economic controls under the guiding hand of an enlightened and well meaning government. However, most people content with the ever-improving economy did not want to tamper with a good thing. They did not pay much attention, at least not until the depression in the early part of the 20th century.

In the 1930s another depression of major proportions hit. As was the case with prior depressions, people felt a sense of helplessness and sought a solution. They listened to the critics of the free market, and were willing to take a small step in the direction of government control over the economy. Like the first step toward a free market this move was limited. It was a Keynesian revolution. The controls and regulations were mild and the government worked within the basic framework of a market economy. New sources of demand were opened up and, as a huge supply infrastructure still existed, a marvelous and undreamed of period of abundance resulted. This was the transitional phase to a controlled economy.

After a while, these controls and regulations impeded the workings of the market place and demand began to outpace supply, setting off inflation. Prices rose and rose and then rose some more until it seemed like they would never be able to fall again. This spiraling inflation defined the 1970s and the Carter years. In frustration, people turned to Ronald Reagan and the Republicans, who made a valiant effort to resurrect laissez-faire economics and the élan of the capitalist. But the deck was stacked against them. Although they cooled the inflation and brought back some of the old capitalist spirit, much of the new entrepreneurial drive directed itself toward rearranging existing wealth (e.g., restructuring businesses, leveraged buy outs, and arbitraging).

It is clear that since the beginning of the Middle Ages, there have been two and a half cycles, wherein Western society went from economic freedom to economic regulation and back again. Each cycle began when the government removed the shackles from commerce, so the economy could develop unencumbered. The economic freedom encouraged savings and investment, and as a result, a remarkable and sustained period of economic growth followed. During this time there is a tendency toward lower prices. This is a supply side economy, meaning supply is greater than demand and prices remain low. It usually lasts 100 to 200 years.

Supply Side Characteristics

This period is usually characterized by a cultural fresh-
ness and originality. Large numbers of people born of
modest means, but showing courage, ambition, and talent,
climb the ladder of social mobility into the middle class. A
vast expansion of the boundaries of liberty occurs, encouraged by the increased economic freedom that results from
limiting the power of the state.

Strongly held religious beliefs and their associated values,
such as industry, temperance, and frugality, normally aid
and abet a period of commercial freedom. Although the
particular system of values will differ at different times,
generally, they offer a path for people to overcome their
animal-like nature and *earn* their dignity. The values
offered by religion play an important role in guiding behavior. Religion often asks people to put aside selfish
aims, accept authority, and recognize the legitimacy of
certain traditional institutions. If people answer this call,
politicians can rely on religion to apply the restraint to
human behavior, freeing the government from the business of political and economic control.

Generally, after about 100 to 200 years of commercial
freedom serious problems appear. The increasing prosperity fuels materialistic values that emphasize self-realiza-
tion and the gratification of one's appetites. This new set
of worldly values eats away at the older values, which had
provided the self-discipline and civic spirit to underpin
our economic and social system. The gap between rich and
poor widens, antagonizing those who were left behind. An
extremely competitive economic atmosphere frightens
many members of the advantaged classes. The ceaseless

pace of advancement arouse⁻ 　 ⁻ t deal of anxiety. People come to a general agre⁻ 　 o call in a referee—the government—to mitigate th⁻ ⁻ffects of the economic and social changes and to reestablish order. The upper classes want to defend their positions, while the lower classes want more protection and security—but they both seek government intervention.

Government Steps In

Periods of increasing government intervention also seem to last about 200 years. During these periods the government focuses on stabilizing the economy, curbing competition, and offering more opportunities to the poor and powerless. The politicians increase people's purchasing power and this produces a demand side economy. Its unintended consequence is a disincentive to working, saving and investment, which limits the economy's ability to spew out the massive increases in supply that were achieved in the period past. In this supply-constrained economy we usually experience a slower rate of economic growth, very modest increases at best in living standards, and vastly increased inflationary pressures. There are, of course, Kondratief upswings during these periods, but they are usually more modest than during a period of commercial freedom. The winners during these times are mostly those closely connected to the governing authorities, or financiers who are quick to learn how to reallocate the existing wealth. The creators of new wealth are less numerous.

In general, *especially after the transition period,* this period is a time of troubles. The government becomes all-powerful, through its attempts to provide the stability and security sought by the public. Some of the recently gained personal liberties are sacrificed. The politicians set up a vast and powerful central bureaucracy to administer increasingly complex rules and regulations. As time passes, these agencies become more inefficient, and abuses of its power more numerous. We enter an age which the German sociologist, Max Weber, called, "The iron age of bureaucratic bondage."

Materialistic values that glorify a "do your own thing" ethic, are in the driver's seat. Human dignity is no longer something people must earn; rather, it is something the state *owes* them. People question authority and the inherent legitimacy of society's institutions. Individuals feel it is their right to decide which of society's rules to follow and which to flout. These attitudes fuel a breakdown of social order, and further the need for increased government control. Finally, after a long downhill slide in the standard of living people lose hope that the material condition of their life will ever improve. At the same time growing numbers of people become thoroughly revolted by the excesses resulting from the new values. They are ready to ride the wave of a new and uplifting religious revival, which preaches the postponement of immediate gratification for the sake of some higher and more enduring satisfaction. This helps set the stage for another economic regeneration. It is interesting to note England, which experienced a Puritan revolution in the late 17th century, turned its energies to fostering an industrial revolution in the following century. In contrast, its chief commercial rival, France, which did not undergo a religious revival, continued to channel its energies into storming the barricades of the established institutions and traditions, while the privileged classes continued on their merry high spending, loose living ways—until finally in 1789 the society cracked wide open.

The Next 35 Years

Let us suppose that this description of the Western world, alternating between economic freedom and government control, is essentially correct. The period beginning in the 1990s would most likely go something like this: After cooling the inflation of the 1970s once and for all, and working off the excesses of the last expansionary phase, we try to begin the next Kondratieff upswing and meet the problem of inflation head on. Only this time the infrastructure of a supply-side economy is not there to hold inflationary pressures in check. Inflation rears its head early in the up wave.

This will be the first time that we have to cope with the problem of inflation and increasing social disorder within the framework of a democratic government. In the demand side economies of the 14th and 17th century, people did not have a vote, while in the 1970s we were still in a transitional period. And this is quite scary. Plato warned about the dangers inherent in democracy. He was quite concerned about democracy as a viable form of government primarily because he thought the poor who are in the majority would use their political power to expropriate the wealth of the more affluent minority. He believed these demands would lead to economic chaos, followed by political chaos, until finally, a dictator would restore order.

Let's see how the inflationary scenario may play itself out in a democracy. As the government is unable to stop the inflation and provide economic gains, people lose confidence in their leaders. Politicians mindful of their growing loss of authority try to hang on by attempting to accommodate the various demands, disregarding the long term consequences. This behavior legitimizes people's ever-increasing demands on the state, and finally, people begin to act like an unruly mob. It becomes exceedingly difficult to control behavior. As different classes and groups fight to hang on to their share of the pie, social tensions increase and the fabric of society seems to give way. The politicians respond by making further accommodations to appease the various groups furthering inflation and social disorder even more.

Finally amidst a crisis approximately 100 years after the great depression of the 1930s there is another far-reaching restructuring of the economy. We push to its limit the notion that the government should be responsible for our economic security. The government extends its control over production, jobs and the wealth of society, thus putting the economy in "irons." Also, in order to ameliorate some of the social unrest and restore order some political liberty must be sacrificed.

Politicians Put on the Spot

Inflation in a demand side economy is very difficult to stop, especially so during times of political democracy. Once people have given the government the responsibility to control and guide the economy, politicians must deliver in order to justify their existence. They must keep the economy on an even keel, and satisfy people's expectations for a better life. The very success of that effort makes people feel more secure, but it also breeds ever greater expectations by the public, which carry demands for output far beyond the limits tolerable to the free market. Yet, politicians, if they hope to retain their legitimacy and their political lives, cannot say no, no matter how nonsensical these demands become. Nor can they stand idle and let the market act as a disciplining agent—disposing of inflated and unrealistic expectations by delivering the spanking of a depression—as 19th century politicians could. Instead, they attempt to satisfy the demands of a public that feels entitled to a good life in an economy that is losing its vitality. This causes immense inflationary pressures. And, as history tells us, soaring prices are almost always a prelude to social chaos, and eventually, political upheaval. Ultimately, the government must assert even more control over the economy and human behavior.

The case for a long-term age of inflation, beginning shortly after the turn of the century, is quite strong. Take the end of the oil age: if we are unable to come up with a cheap new energy source, more of our resources will have to be directed into providing energy, less will be available for the actual production of goods and services. That means a higher price for energy along with relatively fewer goods per capita, which is a recipe for inflation.

Once an up wave begins there would likely be upward pressure on energy prices that would quickly flow through the entire world economy. The huge government deficit also suggests inflation. Governments generally do not repudiate debt. Rather, they inflate their way out by depreciating their currency so that in real terms the debt becomes less.

The most notable example was Germany following WW I. Under the terms of the Versailles Peace Treaty, Germany was required to pay the victorious Allies reparations of 132 billion marks—equivalent to half the nation's pre-war wealth. Already saddled with a large debt from financing its war effort, Germany could not make the huge reparation payments. Leftist political parties attained political control of the newly proclaimed Weimar Republic, which had just adopted a Democratic form of government.

However, as Germany lacked the institutional framework necessary to handle democratic rules, the governing parties felt insecure and hence were loathe to impose the harsh economic austerity necessary to meet the country's debt obligations. Instead, the government attempted to accommodate both its citizens' diverse social and economic demands and pay off the nation's war debts. The result was a relentless and accelerating inflation, which was to become the wildest the world has ever known. The value of the mark tumbled and soon even the best paid workers were unable to purchase the barest necessities of life.

Money is the traditional medium of exchange by which status is guaranteed, security attained, and the fruits of one's labor stored. When money loses its value, the institutions of a society break down and with it go the long established middle class values.

A new decadent and desolate generation flocked to Berlin. The city became the Babylon of the modern world, wherein every sort of excess flourished. Order broke down and street battles between the left and the right became a daily affair. By the autumn of 1923, with manufacturing shutting down and farmers holding back their produce, food riots became a daily occurrence. The cost of a loaf of bread or a stamp to mail a letter was in the trillions of marks. In a mad attempt to keep up with the rising prices the government ran the printing presses full blast, day and night, limited only by the fatigue of the printers. Money had, in fact, no value. It cost more to print a note than the note was worth. A pound of butter, on the other hand, had value. It could purchase a pair of boots, a portrait, a semester's schooling and, of course, sex. As money became worthless, those members of the middle class who had trusted the government and saved for their old age or a better life lost their stake in the social order. No doubt, the anger and frustration of the middle class played an important part in the rise of Hitler and the Nazis, and the fall of the traditional politicians.

U.S. Facing Its Own Age of Inflation

The United States is currently in a situation similar to that of other debtor nations. Eventually we may have to actively inflate our way out. There is, however, an important difference between us and the Weimar Republic. We do have strong institutions that support our democracy. As a result, inflation and the corresponding social chaos are not likely to reach the extreme level they did in Germany in the 1920s.

So what should the investor do when faced with an age of inflation? First he should be aware that the shift to a demand side economic framework is changing the way the

Kondratieff wave works. We already saw this during the last cycle. Inflationary stresses are usually felt at two points in the cycle. The first is a stimulative inflation that generally starts shortly before the beginning of the upswing. The second and more difficult inflationary pressure typically surfaces about 15 to 20 years into the expansionary phase. This is the point wherein the tensions inherent in the expansion set off an inflationary outburst. In a laissez-faire economy these inflations ran through the economy in a few years time and quickly burned themselves out. Prices retreated and the economy returned to its normal growth trajectory. However, the Keynesian revolution has changed this pattern. Inflationary interludes were no longer temporary affairs that quickly burned out. Rather they were terrifying and prolonged, lasting a decade or more. They seemed to defy all the laws of economics.

The first modern inflationary interlude began in about 1940. During the following 10 years prices rose by a whopping 75 percent. This inflation began while the economy was still in its depressionary phase and placed a floor under the downward movement of the economy. As a result, the economy climbed out of depression earlier than usual. The second inflationary interlude began in about mid-1971 and was even more pronounced. By mid-1981 prices had soared 133 percent and a 1971 dollar was worth only 43 cents. It was the nation's most protracted period of inflation in more than a century. Savers were beaten up on and people's confidence in the economy's ability to generate productive wealth was shot.

Both the intense inflation of the 1940s and the 1970s lasted for about a decade. During these times people

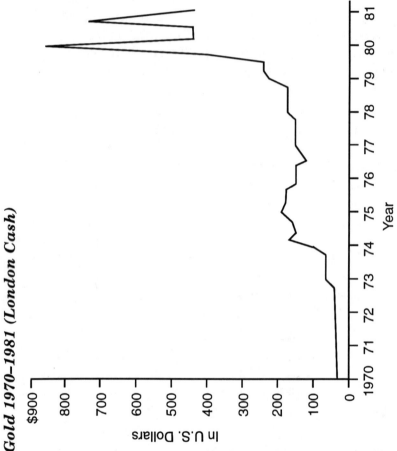

Figure 14–1 Gold 1970–1981 (London Cash)

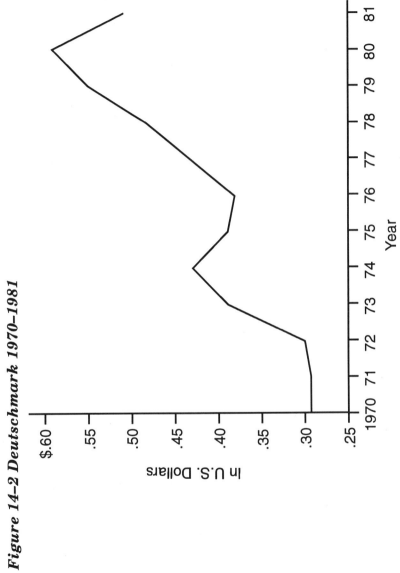

Figure 14-2 Deutschmark 1970–1981

changed their spending and investment habits in ways that ensured inflation would take on a self-feeding character. When people caught on to the fact that the purchasing power of their money was falling, they adopted a "buy now and beat the price increase" mentality. They also sought refuge for their savings in gold and Swiss francs, or diamonds and antiques, because they have speculative possibilities vastly preferable to the investment in productive plant and equipment that the nation needed. The result was a diversion of savings from productive investment into the byways and back alleys of investment.

The productive power of the economy fell still further, and this widened the discrepancy between the output of goods and consumer demand even more. In the first inflationary period, the extended stimulative inflation appeared to moderate the depression and cut short the length of the Kondratieff down wave. In the second period, the long inflationary interlude seemed to throw the economy into a stall for a number of years, and by so doing, extended the length of the up phase.

Inflation Sends Investors Searching for Real Assets

During periods of galloping inflation, the dominant force in investment markets becomes an unquenchable thirst for real assets. Gold, commodities, real estate, collectibles, foreign currencies, all march to the tune of a spiraling price level, while stocks and bonds falter. The investment strategy is simple: get out of stocks and bonds and load up on hard assets and foreign currencies. During the last inflationary episode in the 1970s, the price of gold began the period at about $40 an ounce and soared to $850 (see

Figure 14–1); silver skyrocketed from $1.50 per ounce to $50; a barrel of oil went from $1.50 to about $45; sugar beginning at 5 cents a pound soared to 66 cents; the CRB index marched from 100 to 340; and the DM went from about 29 cents to the mark to 58 cents to the same mark (see Figure 14–2).

This is to say nothing about collectibles, such as art, antiques, coins and other tangible items that tripled in price—in fact, quadrupled in some cases, and in a few cases rose more than ten-fold. Clearly gargantuan moves, these price performances provided investors with a great deal more opportunity than the traditional investments of stocks and bonds. In fact, from mid-1971 to mid-1981 the stock market was down approximately 1 percent, while long-term interest rates soared from about 7 percent to almost 16 percent, which meant holders of long-term bonds suffered huge losses as the value of the bond plummeted.

While there are many tangible investments to choose from, gold and Deutsche marks seem to be the two surest bets. Gold has a long history of tracking the price level. For instance, it is claimed that one ounce of gold bought two men's suits in 1780, and 200 years later, in the early 1980s, that same ounce of gold still bought two men's suits. The Deutsche mark also is a good bet, as a result of the great inflation Germany experienced following World War I. Germans will never forget that period. To them it was a lesson of pain, far surpassing the effects of the great depression. Consequently, Germany pursues policies that emphasize tight money, a strong currency, and a high savings rate, so as not to repeat this experience.

Periods of rampant inflation drag on and on until most people, including the economists, begin to think that moderate price behavior has permanently disappeared. But inflation does cool off and settle back into a more moderate pace, for a while at least. Before this cooling off occurs, however, interest rates are driven much higher and the public becomes so fed up with what is going on that they are willing to return to an Administration that is dedicated to stopping the continual price increases.

Once these inflations cool, investment opportunities in non-conventional assets basically disappear and the stock and real estate markets put in the best performances until another outbreak of galloping inflation begins. (Following the second inflation of the Kondratieff cycle, long-term bonds are also a good investment.)

Stock Market Weaker in 21st Century

If my assessment that we are in an age of inflation is correct, it is entirely possible that the stock market will not be the prime investment vehicle that it was during the 20th century. This is because during the past 100 years we were in either a supply side or transitional economy that churned out enormous increases in productive wealth. However, during the next century we will have entered a period when entrepreneurial drive is directed toward rearranging the existing wealth rather than creating new wealth. If this is so, the rewards from investing in stocks may be significantly less than they were in the 20th century. There is a distinct possibility that the century-long period wherein stocks significantly outperformed other investments may be coming to an end. Sure the Dow may sell at 10,000 or above during the first quarter of the next century, but this may well be in depreciated dollars.

To gauge the inflationary pressures in the economy there are a number of other factors to keep an eye on. First, are we getting the Democrats, at a time when we need the Republicans, say during the first or third stage of an up phase? If so, their policies might feed inflation. Second, has the independence of the Fed been curtailed? Without this bulwark against inflation it is unlikely we will be able to muster the will to stop the rapid price rise? Third, watch out for price indexing. If we begin to price index, it means we are institutionalizing inflation and it will become even more difficult to stop. Finally, if we are unable to find a new and cheap source of fuel, it could very well be that some other nation will. In that case, the pressure on us to maintain our military position will be immense and will likely propel huge expenditures.

There is a very real possibility that in the next century we will encounter an age of inflation and Kondratieff cycles will be different. Inflation will be calling the tune. In this scenario it means that during the up waves inflation will be mind boggling, perhaps reaching triple digits. If so, gold, foreign currencies, and hard assets will most likely be much more profitable than stocks. We could easily see gold prices in the thousands, perhaps $5,000 an ounce or more. On the other hand, stocks, in inflation-adjusted returns, should lag. The prices of homes in good areas could reach astronomical levels, and interest rates could very well rise to heights that would seem unimaginable today.

Chapter Fourteen

The world and the economy are changing once more. Perhaps we should heed the advise of the chorus in the Greek play *Antigone*. "Not only do men move about on an uncharted landscape. The landscape itself is in constant motion, and men best be quick enough to move about with it. When they aren't, they go through the cracks that open under their feet."

INDEX

● ● ● ● ● ●

Index

Index

Index

Mill, John Stuart, 41
Monarchies, 183-185
Montgomery Ward, 25
Morgan, J.P., 20

N

Napoleon, 74, 78
Napoleonic wars, 76
National Bureau of Economic Research, 87
New Deal, 29
New York Stock Exchange, 24
Nixon, Richard, 54, 56, 115-117, 119
Nuclear
  fusion, 141
  power, 138, 139

O

100-year
  cycle, 65, 68-70, 77, 123, 135, 154
  revolution, 67, 73
Office buildings, 104
Oil age
  end, 135-147
  winners, 146-147
Oil shortage, 143
Optimism, 46, 47, 94, 110, 173
  see Economic, Overoptimism
  error, 6-7, 47
  mass psychology, 84
Overexpansion, 80
Overextension, 25
Overoptimism, 175, 176
Owen, Robert

P

Parliamentary reform, 38
Performance, 25
Pessimism, 90, 94, 121, 123
  error, 10-12, 30
  psychology, 84
Plateau period, 7
Political factors, 97-105, 193-196
Pool operators, 24
Poverty, 24
Present cycle, 51-64
Price(s), 43
  see Assets, Bonds, Land, Real estate, Stock
  controls, 116
  level, 23
Products, see Consumer
Production, see Industrial
Productivity, 7, 20, 23, 154-156
  see Labor
Profit, 6, 8, 14, 18, 38, 43, 109, 154-156
  margin, 23, 43, 109
Profitability, 8, 26, 155
Progress, 43
Prohibition, 17
Prosperity, 2, 3, 5, 10, 13, 18, 22, 26-28, 35, 37, 39, 41, 46, 49, 66, 84-86, 89
Protectionism, 182-183
Psychological
  beings, 83
  change, 87
  environment, 86
Purchases, 8
Purchasing power, 78
  see Consumer
Puritanism, 18, 70-73, 75

Index